Institute of Contemporary British History
Cairncross Treasury Series

The Control of
Demand 1958–1964

Russell Bretherton

Institute of Contemporary British History
Senate House, University of London
Malet Street, London WC1E 7HU

© Crown copyright. Reproduced with the permission of the Controller of Her Majesty's Stationery Office.

Published by the Institute of Contemporary British History 1999

ISBN: 0 9523210 2 5

T

Typeset in 10 point Times by the Institute of Contemporary British History

Printed and bound by Biddles Ltd

Contents

Foreword

Russell Bretherton (1906–92) was in pre-war years an academic economist teaching economics and modern history at Wadham College, Oxford, where he was a Fellow from 1925 to 1945. In his last three years there (1936–39) he held a research appointment, one fruit of which was the publication in 1942 of *Public Investment and the Trade Cycle*, written jointly with Burchardt and Rutherford. During the war he served as an under-secretary in the Raw Materials Department of the Ministry of Supply, moving to similar duties in the Board of Trade once the war was over. In 1949 he joined the Economic Section under Robert Hall until he was posted in 1951 to the newly created and short-lived Ministry of Materials. He then entered the Treasury in 1961, still as under-secretary, and remained there until his retirement in 1968. It was shortly before his retirement that he was commissioned to write a sequel to Holmans's work on demand management in the 1950s with a study of subsequent experience between 1958 and 1964.

His study of demand management was completed by 1968 although the copy of it used for publication in this series was dated 1972. We are grateful to the Treasury for giving us a copy to work from. It was based exclusively on Treasury files coupled with some consultations with colleagues in the Treasury. Ministers, so far as I am aware, had no opportunity of seeing and commenting on the text. How Bretherton would regard his monograph now it is impossible to say. But perhaps, as he can no longer comment on his findings, I may offer some personal comments as the Government's Economic Adviser from 1961 to 1964.

Bretherton provides a useful critique of demand management in the concluding years of Conservative Government from 1958 to 1964. He also reviews the handling of incomes policy and the reliability of the forecasts made by the Treasury. His interest is largely in what happened at the official level. But since ministers have to take responsibility for policy it is important not to lose sight of their part in the story and in particular the role of the Prime Minister, Harold Macmillan, whose strong bias towards an expansionary policy was repeatedly manifested in those years. It was a bias shared neither by Heathcoat Amory (Chancellor of the Exchequer 1958-60) nor by Selwyn Lloyd (Chancellor of the Exchequer in 1960-63) but was in close keeping with the inclinations of Reginald Maudling who became Chancellor in July 1962. No one reading the exchange of correspondence between Maudling and Macmillan in early July 1962 can doubt that it played a part in the removal from office of Selwyn Lloyd although I was told a different story at the time by the Prime Minister's secretary, Sir Timothy Bligh. This laid emphasis on Selwyn Lloyd's failure to take the lead in introducing a long-term incomes policy and so obliging the Prime Minister to take that responsibility. The departure of Heathcoat Amory from the Treasury two years earlier may also have been associated with the over-expansion initiated in 1959 in spite of Heathcoat Amory's strong inclination to a cautious policy.

In an assessment of the depression of 1962 it is also necessary to give proper weight to the effects of the sharp fall on Wall Street in May. This heralded a marked change in the business climate in the second half of the year which took officials and forecasters by surprise. The Board of Trade had insisted that exports in 1962 would show a 9 per cent increase and the forecasters in the Treasury had been obliged to build this estimate into their forecast with no confidence in it. The actual increase was under 3 per cent, even at current prices, and only half what it had been in each of the previous two years.

But it is 1964 that is most puzzling. Why did the Government take no action between April and October in spite of an enormous and growing balance of payments deficit, a continuing fall in unemployment to well below 2 per cent and every evidence of a major boom? One reason is the determination of the Government – particularly in the shadow of an election – to avoid anything smacking of 'stop-go'. But there was also the strange behaviour of the index of production which remained unchanged between January and September for nine successive months in 1964 and gave Maudling the impression that the economy was 'stuck'. He had promised his officials in June that he would take restrictive action in July in the form of a call for 'special deposits'; but when July came he felt obliged to renege, letting the deficit in the balance of payments grow to a record peace-time level.

It was all a repetition of what had happened in 1960 when the economy, under similar pressure, sucked in additional imports to meet an expanding demand. It also reflected uncertainty over the figures. While Bretherton was writing, the CSO revised the published figures of industrial production to show a steep climb in 1964 in place of a fixed level. Then, within a year or two, a further revision of the figures restored the original picture. The output index of GDP came to read in successive quarters 70.2, 70.0, and 70.8 as if the economy really was 'stuck'. As Robert Hall used to say: 'The hardest thing to forecast is where you are now'.

There had been an earlier problem over the desirability of aligning movements in British and American interest rates. A proposal was made in December 1963 to raise bank rate by 0.5 per cent. About the same time the clearing banks themselves were pressing to be allowed to charge an extra 1 per cent on overdrafts in order to restore their profit margins. All this became involved with an effort to keep in line with the Federal Reserve Bank and so time changes in interest rates in the United Kingdom as to coincide with changes in the United States. Three months elapsed between the first proposal to raise bank rate and Maudling's final decision to act unilaterally. The attempt to keep in step was never repeated.

Sir Alec Cairncross

Calendar of Persons

Prime Minister

Harold Macmillan	January 1957–October 1963
Sir Alec Douglas-Home	October 1963–October 1964

Chancellor of the Exchequer

D. Heathcoat-Amory	January 1958–27 July 1960
John Selwyn Brook Lloyd	27 July 1960–13 July 1962
Reginald Maudling	13 July 1962–October 1964

Joint Permanent Secretary to the Treasury

Sir Roger Makins	1956–December 1959
Sir Frank Lee	January 1960–October 1962
Sir William Armstrong	October 1962–1968

Second Secretaries, Treasury

Sir Denis Rickett	1954–68
Sir Thomas Padmore	1952–62
R W B Clarke	1962–66

Economic Adviser to HMG

Sir Robert Hall	1953–May 1961
Sir Alec Cairncross	June 1961–October 1964

Introduction

The course of the economy

This study covers the period of just over six years from the summer of 1958 to the autumn of 1964. As compared with the six years before, and with the six years after, this was a period of growth in the British economy. The gross national product in 1964 was, measured at constant prices, some 26 per cent above that of 1958[1]: an average cumulative growth of 4 per cent a year. From 1952 to 1958 the increase was only some 16 per cent from 1964 to 1970 it was again about 16 per cent. It is true that 1958 was a year of some industrial recession, whereas 1964 was near the peak of a boom. It is also true that the working population, and also the total population,[2] in the United Kingdom, rose by about 4.5 per cent in the period, so that the growth in average production, and in average real income, per head was rather smaller; and it was also markedly less than in most of the developed countries of western Europe, though not much less than that in the United States. It was, nonetheless, probably a faster growth in real income per head than had been achieved in Britain for any period of similar length during the twentieth century. It is necessary to emphasise this because during most of the period the keynote was impatience and criticism both of the nation's performance and of the Government' s management of the economy, by 'stop and go.'

These are quantitative assessments. The measuring rods used take little account of changes, up or down, in the quality of goods produced, and still less of changes in the quality of services rendered and in the general environment for living. Whether on balance these improved or deteriorated during the period is a matter for personal opinion rather than statistical measurement. The prices of services generally rose considerably relatively to those of manufactured goods, because the opportunities for rendering given amounts of them with less labour were smaller than in manufacture. Public consumption consists disproportionately of services, and this accounts for part of the growth in the relative importance of public expenditure, which is referred to later. Personal spending power also probably became more evenly distributed during the period, but this is referred to only incidentally in this study.

The growth of the economy was, indeed, not even. The period began with an industrial recession which reached its lowest point in the third quarter 1958. Thereafter there were two years of rapid recovery, flattening out to another shallow recession from the autumn of 1961 to the end of 1962. This was followed by another rapid expansion which continued, though with falling momentum, through 1965 until the summer of 1966. These fluctuations were not, however, large by any standards. In no year did the gross national product measured at constant prices fall below that of the preceding year, as it had done in 1952 and in 1958; and the largest increase in any year – 1964 on 1963 – was under 5.5 per cent. Even the index of manufacturing production, which covered the most variable part, did not fall for any calendar year: its largest increases were about 6 per cent for 1960 above 1959 and 8 to 9 per cent for 1964 above 1963.[3] The averages of monthly registered unemployed in the United Kingdom[4] moved down from 500,000 (2.2 per cent) for 1958 to 377,000 (1.6 per cent) for 1961, and up again to 612,000 (2.6 per cent) for 1963; for 1964 they fell back to 413,000 (1.7 per cent.), and to 360,000 (1.5 per cent) for 1965. The seasonal extremes were, of course, wider than this: below 300,000 in July 1961, but above 600,000 only in January 1959 and in the abnormal winter weather of January to March 1963. The lowest points of unemployment were considerably higher than in the earlier years: in 1954, 1955 and 1956 the monthly averages had been around 1.3 per cent, 1.2 per cent, 1.3 per cent. The high year 1963, at 2.6 per cent, was higher than 1953 and 1958. Accentuation of problems of structural and regional unemployment was one of the disturbing features of the period. The total numbers employed,[5] however, as shown by the June counts, rose in every year from 1959 to 1964; there were no absolute setbacks, like those recorded in 1958 and again in 1968, 1969 and 1970.

This substantial growth in the national product was accompanied by a rise in costs and prices slightly larger than that during the previous six years though not nearly as rapid as that experienced between 1964 and 1970. Taking total final prices of goods sold on the home market[6] as the broadest measure (1958=100) this rise was 14.1 per cent to 1964. Though continuous, it was uneven. Only 2 points in the first two years, it jumped by 6 points in 1961 and 1962, slackened in 1963, and rose again sharply in 1964. This was essentially a domestic inflation; the prices of imported goods and services rose by only 7 points, almost all in the last two years. The index of retail prices[7] rose by more than that of final output, by about 16 per cent after allowing for changes in its base and weighting, mainly because it was heavily weighted by rents, which were partly decontrolled in 1958, and by drink and tobacco, which bore the brunt of successive increases in indirect taxation. Thus gross national product as a whole rose from 1958 to 1959 in money terms by about £9,000 million – 44 per cent; but nearly half of this represented a fall in the value of money. This is the most obvious failure of economic management during the period, and it was the precursor of similar but greater failure in the next six years.

It has been, and can still be, disputed how far this inflation might have been prevented or reduced by fiercer Government control of demand and of the money supply. The partial dichotomy between Government policy in control of demand and in its incomes policy is indeed one the themes of this study. But it is beyond reasonable doubt that the main dynamic was the continuous, if variable, pressure to increase rates of wages and salaries faster than the actual growth of production per person employed, averaged over the whole economy. There are some difficulties, both practical and philosophical, in measuring this growth precisely; but it certainly did not exceed 20 per cent in real terms between 1958 and 1964, even after discounting the fact that much of the increased employment was female or part time. Yet the average weekly money earnings (including overtime) of male manual workers rose by about 36 per cent, and the average weekly hours worked fell from 48.2 to 46.9; hourly wage-rates for all workers rose by about 31 per cent.[8] It was this discrepancy between the rise of wages and of productivity which accounted for most of the calculated increase of 14–16 per cent in the rise of home costs per unit of output.

The second major failure was to secure any margin of safety in the balance of external payments. This was, of course, no new problem. There had been crises or near-crises of strain on sterling in 1952, in the summer of 1955, after the Suez affair in 1956, and again in August and September 1957; they were repeated in 1960 and in 1961, and in November 1964. All these were met by measures which included fiscal restraint of internal demand as well as use of the ordinary monetary instruments; but their very frequency, combined with the speed with which the immediate strain on the exchange rates was relieved, disguised the underlying causes and also had a deadening effect on the attitude of the public and of many ministers and officials. Few took seriously, for long at a time, the Treasury (OF) doctrine that a surplus of £350 million on current account, to cover net investment abroad and to build up the reserves, ought to be a precondition for expanding the economy. Such a surplus was, in fact, realised in 1958 (£344 million),[9] and sterling was made convertible at the end of that year. The surplus was still respectable, at £143 million, in 1959, but it fell steeply into deficit (-£265 million) during the boom of 1960. The current balance was level in 1961, and showed surpluses of over £100 million in 1962 and in 1963, before collapsing again to a deficit in 1964 of which £381 million seems to be the latest calculation.

Exports of goods and services grew in every year after 1958 (when they had fallen) though never fast enough. The main trouble came from the wild gyrations of imports. In 1958 imports, valued fob, were actually below the levels of the previous three years. In 1959 and 1960 they rose by £260 million and again by £500 million – a jump of nearly one quarter in the two years. They fell back somewhat in 1961 and 1962, rose by £367 million in 1963, and broke all records with a further jump of £643 million in 1964. The main cause of this erratic behaviour was stocking and de-stocking in the up-swings and down-swings of the industrial cycle, small though these were in themselves: but in 1964 the rise was certainly accentuated by higher prices and perhaps by attempts to beat the gun of import restrictions, surcharges, or devaluation of sterling. The fluctuations were the despair of the forecasters; and they made it impossible to diagnose with certainty whether the underlying propensity to import was, or was not, more than we could afford to pay for by exports and other sources of foreign earnings. There was less doubt about the trend of some other debits in the current balance, such as the rise of Government expenditure overseas from £276 million in 1958 to £477 million in 1964 and the sluggishness of our *net* earnings from shipping; but these were in themselves relatively small items.

The current balance was of course only part of the story. The balance of long-term capital transactions, so far as they could be identified, was also highly erratic, varying from a credit of £68 million in 1961 to debits of £255 million in 1959 and £363 million in 1964. British private investment abroad was fairly steady around £300 million a year, except for a drop in 1962 and a jump to £400 million in 1964; and movements in it could be foreseen and to some extent influenced through the exchange control. Foreign private investment in the UK grew very helpfully over the period as a whole, but varied much more from year to year; a sudden rise of £200 million helped to provide the net long-term credit of 1962, but a fall of £125 million in 1964 contributed to the other troubles of that year. There was also the balancing item of unidentified transactions, needed to equate the known credits or debits with the *net* totals of monetary movements. As finally calculated, this was small in most years, but there is still an enormous credit under that head in 1960 of £299 million, for which, despite more than one attempt on the files, there seems to be no satisfactory explanation. Except in that year, and in 1964, movements of the current and of the long-term capital balances tended fortuitously but fortunately to offset one another, and the overall balance of payments for the other whole years was not far from equilibrium, though the period began with an overall surplus of £148 million in 1958.

Another development relevant to the control of demand was the disproportionate growth of expenditure by the public sector – central government, local authorities, public corporations.[10] While, as we have seen, the gross national product rose, in money terms, by about 44 per cent from 1958 to 1964, expenditure by the public sector (including grants to the private sector) grew by nearly 54 per cent, and by 1964 it equalled 43.7 per cent of the gross national product, instead of only 40.7 per cent in 1958. Of its major constituents, fixed investment grew fastest – by nearly three-quarters – largely because of housing and the massive electricity programme; and current expenditure on goods and services by over a half. Grants (largely social security benefits) grew by 60 per cent. These were not, of course, a direct claim on productive resources; but they almost certainly increased consumption by more than it was held back by the taxes and contributions raised to finance them. Debt interest, which may have worked in the opposite way, increased least of all, by under a third and by 1964 was little over one tenth of all public expenditure. Within this total, budgetary expenditure by the central government (above and below the line) rose by about £2,700 million, nearly 47 per cent.[11]

Paradoxically, the growing importance of public expenditure, especially on fixed investment, probably during this period increased the difficulties of controlling demand and the economy. Cuts were made at the crises of restraint; but politically these proved even more awkward than imposing more taxation, and some of their actual effects on spending only materialised, as in 1958 and 1962, when stimulus, rather than restraint, was required. In periods of reflation, it was easy and popular to authorise large increases in programmes, as was done in the autumns of 1958 and 1962; but their implementation mostly came when the economy was again in need of restraint in 1961 and 1964. During this period at least, counter-cyclical variation of public expenditure was not successful. The underlying need to impose more taxation to cover the rise in expenditure also made it more difficult to use fiscal weapons to restrain demand as well, and caused awkward problems of financing when tax remissions were used to expand it, as in 1959 and 1963.

Finally, one must note the effect of the large changes in the structure and location of industry and transport. The gaps between the levels of employment and of incomes in the south and Midlands on the one side, and much of the rest of the country on the other, widened markedly during the period. This meant that low unemployment and pressure on resources in the south and Midlands coexisted with high unemployment and stagnation in many places elsewhere; the average came to mean less and less. This much increased the difficulty of applying measures of restraint which were mainly nationwide in their effect; and not much progress was made in developing measures which could be geographically selective, either for restraint or for expansion, but at the same time consistent with general control.

The big structural changes, which overlapped with the locational problems, also increased the difficulties of control. Employment in coal-mining fell from 700,000 in 1958 to 600,000 in 1964; in agriculture from 650,000 to 500,000; on the railways from 500,000 to 396,000; in shipbuilding from 320,000 to 227,000.[12] These changes were, in total, as much due to capital investment and modernisation of methods as to declining demand for the products of these industries. The consequent release of labour was a necessary preliminary to its redeployment elsewhere, with higher productivity and often higher earnings for individuals; and in the end it contributed to the rise in average productivity in the whole economy. But it raised the level of unemployment at any one time, and much of it took place in the times of slackening demand, when reabsorption was most difficult, as well as in awkward places. And, during this period, very little was done, beyond some extension of retraining facilities, either to make re-employment easier or to ease the difficulties of change for individuals and so to make it more acceptable.

Notes

1 Annual Abstract of Statistics 1968, Table 308.
2 *Ibid.*, Tables 128 and 6.
3 Annual Abstract of Statistics 1966, Table 154 and 1969. The indexes based on 1958 and on 1963 weights give somewhat differing results for 1964. The longest growth over a twelve-month period was about 12 per cent March 1959 / February 1960 and January 1963 / December 1963.
4 *Ibid.*, Tables 143 and 144.
5 *Ibid.*, Table 129.
6 National Income and Expenditure 1967, Table 16.
7 Annual Abstract of Statistics 1966, Table 379.
8 *Ibid.*, Table 153.
9 Annual Abstract of Statistics 1968, Table 273.
10 National Income and Expenditure 1967, Table 52.
11 Annual Abstract of Statistics 1968, Table 309.
12 *Ibid.*, 1966, Table 133.

I

Reflation and the Budget of 1959

The long struggle to control the boom which had developed in 1954 and 1955 really ended with the year 1957. There were three crises for sterling, a series of restrictive budgets beginning with the second budget of 1955, increases in bank rate, which reached 7 per cent in September 1957, a drastic use of hire-purchase restrictions, and finally the resignation of the Chancellor (Thorneycroft); and the two Junior Treasury ministers on 6 January 1958, because the Cabinet refused to put public expenditure in a straitjacket. But by that time the boom was indeed broken. Investment and industrial production were falling and unemployment was beginning to rise.

The struggle had, however, distressing effects on the economy. The gross domestic product had risen in real terms by only 2.6 per cent in three years, and manufacturing production by rather less; but nonetheless there had been a steep rise in wages, in unit costs, and in prices. In the later stages the need to stop inflation and to restore confidence in the pound had become the main immediate object of Government policy, taking precedence over the maintenance of full employment or economic growth. The Committee on Prices, Productivity and Incomes, which had been appointed in August 1957, in its first report in February 1958 recommended still more deflation of demand to achieve this aim. Even after Mr Thorneycroft's resignation there was great caution for some time about taking any reflationary measures. Treasury notes for the new Chancellor, Mr Heathcoat Amory, gave the general impression that the pressure on resources had not eased *very much* since the September measures, and the Economic Adviser (Sir Robert Hall) poured some contempt on a public prophesy by Sir Oliver Franks (then Chairman of Lloyds Bank) that 'by June HMG will be begging the banks to expand their advances'.[1]

Mr Heathcoat Amory's first budget, on 15 April, reduced taxation by £100 million and raised the initial allowances on industrial investment. But 'inflation is still the enemy', and for the time being the other September measures of restriction remained in force.

Almost immediately after the budget the climate changed. The Cabinet still, apparently, especially the Prime Minister (Mr Macmillan) took fright at the rising unemployment: the figures for July were 140,000 above those for a year earlier, though still only 2 per cent. Within the Treasury, Sir Robert Hall came out in favour of expansion, though with the important proviso that it ought to be accompanied by a more positive Government policy on wages. In a minute to Sir Roger Makins (then Permanent Secretary) of 8 May he wrote:

Our policy is that we should resume expansion (so far as the position of the pound allows) when we feel more confident about the outlook for wages and prices ... We ought now to be taking the first cautious steps towards expansion. But the Government would look rather silly, and would miss an opportunity, unless it said something more positive about wages. The ideal would be if they would accept some form of 'guiding light', announcing from time to time the amount of wage increases which it thinks consistent with price stability. Could we discuss with the Chancellor?[2]

This recommendation had already been made in January by an interdepartmental committee of officials, and had then been rejected by ministers; and it seems that the Chancellor was not prepared to revive it in May. Nevertheless, reflation was begun without it. Before the end of the month the Budget Committee was actively considering possible fiscal measures to give a quick stimulus to consumer spending, such as paying out post-war credits or an emergency cut in income tax. Though these ideas were not then followed up, during the later stages of the Finance Bill in June the initial allowances for investment in machinery and buildings were raised to 30 per cent. Bank rate was cut from 7 per cent to 5.5 per cent on 22 May, with later reductions which brought it down to 4 per cent by November; and in July the ceilings on bank advances were removed. In July a new drive was announced to encourage industrial investment in the Development Districts, and in August and later the curbs which had been imposed on public sector investment programmes by the September 1957 measures were relaxed. In September and October the restrictions on hire purchase were first reduced and then removed altogether, though power to reimpose them was retained – much to the disgust of the Board of Trade, which had to face their intense unpopularity with the motor and other industries, the growth of whose markets they had restricted. In retrospect, it seems that the removal of hire purchase restrictions was the most effective single reflationary device used on this occasion.

At this stage of reflation, action was rather rough and ready. The July NIF Forecasts showed the presence of considerable slack in the economy and a prospect of more to come, though the emphasis was rather on the need to take up unemployment caused by more efficient use of labour than on the danger of an actual recession. In presenting this report to the Chancellor, Sir Robert Hall wrote: 'I consider that by next year we shall be making less than optimum use of resources, and that there is a clear case for expansion';[3] and he suggested a stimulus to consumption of perhaps £100 million over 12 months, to be secured by relating restrictions on hire purchase and obstacles to spending on house maintenance. These were modest but relatively quick-acting remedies, and he warned against stimulating public investment, which was 'slow to start and hard to stop'. But, once a policy of reflation was known to be accepted, pressures came from all sides, and not least from spending departments and their ministers. Little attempt was made to assess the total effect, or to choose between slow and quick-acting instruments.

Treasury officials generally urged caution about increases of public expenditure. The Chancellor himself went on record to his colleagues in October as favouring 'the bringing forward of expenditure, but only provided that it will not raise the level for 1960 and 1961'; and on 19 December, in a discussion with the Governor of the Bank of England[4] he said definitely that 'quite enough has been done for the time being' – a view with which the Governor agreed. Nevertheless, with reflation as the accepted policy, the stage was being set for an energetic use of fiscal stimulus in the budget of 1959, which was widely expected to precede a general election later in the year.

The NIF Forecast for 1959,[5] published early in December, was a depressing document and gave support to the need for a second round of reflationary measures. Although it took account of what had been done already, it foresaw an increase of consumers' expenditure of only 2.5 per cent, and that mostly early in the year and flattening out as the effects of the relaxation of hire purchase restrictions wore off. Fixed investment would rise by only a similar percentage, and there would be an increase of gross national product of only some £370 million at 1957 factor cost – about 1.5 per cent.

We think it unlikely that unemployment will fall in 1959...It may rise less than it did in 1958, but the recent seasonally corrected increase of about 15,000 a month could well continue in the early months and then be followed by a period of approximate stability.

It concluded that, with present policies, production at the end of 1959 could still be running a least 5 per cent below 'normal potential'. It is obvious in retrospect that this was much too gloomy a view. But the report was written at, or only just after, the up-turn of the economy, and it shows very well the difficulties which beset forecasters at the moment of a change of trend, especially in estimating probable changes in demand for stock-building and work-in-progress. Sir Robert Hall, in a comment for the Budget Committee,[6] concluded that there was need for substantial budget concessions, on top of the other measures already taken and, on the wages/prices aspect, remarked that a 'budget which made some well-judged concessions would be a more important factor making for moderation in wage-settlements than one designed to keep up a high level of unemployment'. He did, however, point to some of the uncertainties: how much further de-stocking would go; how far production would increase without corresponding growth in employment; whether exports might not do better than the decline of £100 million forecast; and whether the easing of credit would check the downward trend of private investment.

The December forecast[7] was revised on 23 February, well before the budget decisions (NIF(WP)(59)2 Final), and was than considerably more optimistic but it still forecast growing slack in the economy. Sir Robert Hall thought that it left things much as they were:

The essence is that reflationary measures so far have given rather more stimulus than expected, but the trend towards economising in labour is also stronger, so that the case for a considerable stimulus remains, especially to have an impact on unemployment.[8]

The Budget Committee at no stage questioned the general diagnosis, or the need for a large remission of taxation. It did, however, stress the importance, on grounds of financial orthodoxy and presentation, especially abroad, of retaining some budget surplus 'above the line'. Its first submission to the Chancellor therefore said that tax concessions of £250/300 million (about 4 per cent of all 1958/59 tax receipts) and 1.75 per cent of consumers' expenditure 'might prove possible and be about right'. At a meeting early in January with Sir Roger Makins and Sir Robert Hall the Chancellor accepted this as a working basis, and also agreed that, although the reduction of income tax must have first priority, there must be broadly equivalent cuts in indirect taxes. Shortly afterwards it was agreed that a hand-out of about £50 of post-war credits might be added, on the ground that this would be 'below-the-line' and would have a once-for-all effect without prejudicing the position for future years. The Inland Revenue, however, then made several increases in their estimates of receipts for 1959/60 and, despite a rise of £237 million in the Supply Estimates (about double the increase between 1957 and 1958/59), the prospective surplus for 1959/60, before tax changes, rose again. The proposed tax concession rose with it; by early March a 'package' which would cost £300 million in 1959/60 and £350 million in a full year was accepted and even bigger figures were being discussed. But the Chancellor himself began to urge caution.[9] He became seriously worried at the size of the overall deficit, then put, after the proposed tax remissions, at around £800 million, which had not figured much in the earlier discussions; and he was also afraid lest, by overdoing the stimulus to the economy, he might create a situation in which taxation had to be increased again in 1960, probably just after a general election. Sir Robert Hall played down his fears on the first point, but supported him on the second, stressing now the 'stiffness' of the economy once it began to swing either up or down, and hence the importance of not doing too many irreversible things. In the end, it was decided not to increase the cut in income tax from 9d to 1s, and to provide for an above-the-line surplus of £100 million and an overall deficit of only £720 million. Nevertheless, the budget presented by Mr Heathcoat Amory on 7 April 1959 made tax concessions expected to cost £295 million in 1959/60 and £360 million in a full year, with, for good measure, a repayment of £71 million of post-war credits as well. This was, both absolutely and relatively to the size of the national product, the biggest budget handout yet in British history (end-war budgets excepted). It considerably exceeded that given by Mr R A Butler in 1953; and, unlike it, it was accompanied by a big increase, instead of some reduction, in supply expenditure.

The standard rate of income tax was reduced from 8/6 (42.5 pence) to 7/9 (38.75 pence) and the lower rates by 6d (2.5 pence). The beer duty was cut by 2d a pint, and most rates of purchase tax by one sixth. There were also concessions on certain motor vehicle duties. In a full year, direct taxation was expected to be reduced by £235 million and indirect taxation by £125 million. Because of the PAYE coding system, it was not until July that income tax deductions from wages and salaries were adjusted downwards and they were thus concentrated in the last nine months of the financial year.

As part of this package, investment allowances were reintroduced, with the hope of giving a stimulus to private investment, largely replacing the initial allowances which had been provided by the Finance Act of 1958. The usual rates became 20 per cent investment allowance plus 10 per cent initial allowance on new plant and machinery, and 10 per cent investment and 5 per cent initial allowance on industrial and agricultural buildings; vehicles and second-hand plant continued to get initial allowances but were given no investment allowance. These changes made little impact on the budget figures for 1959/60, and the Inland Revenue refused to give an estimate of their ultimate cost in the years ahead. They had been the subject of the one serious disagreement among officials about the 1959 budget, which must now be examined.

There were two distinguishable ideas behind the change. The first, which was widely but by no means universally accepted, was that industrial investment made a particularly important contribution to the economy, and that the amount of it was too small, especially in relation to developments of it abroad; it was therefore at any time a fit subject for some fiscal privilege. The second idea, held mainly by economists, was that fiscal stimuli, and also fiscal deterrents, could and should be applied to industrial investment as part of the general policy of controlling demand. When reflation began in the summer of 1958, the Budget Committee set up a special Committee on Incentive Allowances, with Sir Thomas Padmore (then a Second Secretary at the Treasury) in the chair; and this reported early in 1959.[10] Their report distinguished sharply between a) the ordinary writing off of original capital cost by regular annual depreciation allowances, treated as a cost chargeable against gross profits; b) initial allowances, which write off more as a cost in the first year, but less later, so that the total ultimately written off is unaffected; and c) investment allowances, which deduct part of the original cost from taxable profits, but without subsequent diminution of depreciation allowances; so that relief from taxation is given on more than the total cost. Depreciation allowances were not in question, though there could be some argument about the methods applied in calculating them. The Inland Revenue had no objections of principle to initial allowances, but they doubted whether in fact variations in them had much effect on either the amount or the timing of investment. To investment allowances they objected very strongly indeed, on the ground that they involved a subsidy to a particular form of expenditure, and also to particular forms of investment. This, they argued, undermined the equity of income tax as a whole. Investment allowances had in fact been introduced, at 20 per cent for plant and ships and at 10 per cent for buildings, in 1954 but suspended (except for ships), as a measure of restraint in February 1956. Initial allowances had been introduced, at 20 per cent, in 1945; raised to 40 per cent in 1949; abolished in 1952; reinstated at 20 per cent in 1953; and raised to 30 per cent in 1958. The Committee said, no doubt rightly, in view of those gyrations, that no statistical evidence could be found to show that they had had any effect on investment either in the short-term or the long-term; and they quoted the results of an inquiry by the Federation of British Industry in which only a quarter of the firms consulted had said that their investment plans had been affected at all, and some of these had declared that the frequent changes had had a deterrent effect. Two other devices which were adopted in later years, namely 'free depreciation' (i.e. giving firms freedom to choose the date at which they could claim tax relief on the whole value of new investment), and the substitution of outright capital grants for tax allowances, were not seriously considered by the Committee.

The majority of the Committee recommended against the use of investment allowances but not against initial allowances, on grounds of tax principle. They were also lukewarm about the probable effects of either upon the timing of investment, taking the view that this was dominated by fairly short-term views by individual firms about the future demand for their products in relation to their productive capacity. If the outlook for this was unfavourable, decisions to invest would not be taken; if it were favourable, fiscal concessions would not add very much. Sir Robert Hall dissented strongly in a minority note. He attacked the Inland Revenue's distinction of principle; initial allowances were equivalent to an interest-free loan, and were therefore just as much – or as little – a 'subsidy' as that given by investment allowances. In any case, he could not accept that they would distort the equity of income tax any more than existing discriminations in it. As to effects, he thought that once variable investment allowances were introduced and recognised as an instrument of economic policy, firms would soon get used to them and adjust the timing of their investment accordingly; in any case, some stimulus to investment was desirable on general grounds. He did not, however, really dispose of the objection that, because of the time-lag between decisions and spending, such stimuli to investment might well exaggerate rather than reduce its fluctuations.

The Budget Committee on the whole agreed with the majority report; but Sir Roger Makins, in submitting it to the Chancellor,[11] said that he had much sympathy with the minority view, and he suggested as a compromise, which would save money in the longer run, the substitution, partial or complete, of investment allowances for initial allowances. This the Chancellor accepted and implemented in the budget. The division of opinion was not confined to officials. The Federation of British Industry, the National Union of Manufacturers, and the Association of British Chambers of Commerce all asked in their pre-budget representations for the restoration of investment allowances. But the Conservative Party Finance Committee were against it, suggesting consideration of 'free depreciation' instead; and the Economic Secretary (Mr J E S Simon) minuted the Chancellor against it.

The Chancellor set out the aims of his budget in moderate and cautious terms. The prime object of policy was still the maintenance of a stable and strong currency. He had had to satisfy himself that a stimulus to the economy could be justified by the state of the balance of payments on the one side, and, on the other, by the prospect of maintaining stability of prices, 'which had been with much difficulty attained during the past 12 months'. He had concluded that the balance of payments would allow a moderate expansion of imports, which would be a contribution to the re-expansion of world trade after the mild recession of 1958; while for prices the immediate prospects were encouraging, though import prices could rise, and a new round of excessive wage increases could easily push up costs and prices again. The aim of the budget was thus to help to keep the cost of living down and to lower unit costs by encouraging steady but not excessive expansion of production and a continuing high rate of investment. He played down any deliberately reflationary aims; without any reductions in taxation, the above-the-line surplus would be nearly £400 million; this 'was no longer needed', and the surplus of £102 million for which he was providing was enough.[12]

Apart from their general cry of pre-election bribery, the main point made by the Opposition, especially by Mr Wilson, was that tax relief and expansion had been too long delayed, though, somewhat inconsistently, he also attacked the Government for having engineered a consumption boom based on the relaxation of restrictions on hire purchase. Mr Grimond regretted the absence of any selective measures to deal with heavy local pockets of unemployment. Perhaps the most serious criticism came from Mr Enoch Powell on the Government benches; he argued that the overall deficit of £721 million was much too high, and that it must provide a basis for an inflationary growth of bank credit which would be hard to control.

For the rest of 1959 things seemed to go very smoothly. The NIF report at the end of May,[13] taking account both of the budget changes and of recent indicators, was much more cheerful than that of February, but gave no warnings of over-rapid expansion. The rise in consumers' expenditure for 1959 above 1958 was now put at £745 million at current prices (£672 million at 1954 prices), which was more than double the February figure. Industrial production was expected to rise by 5 per cent year to year, and by 6 per cent from fourth quarter to fourth quarter; and gross domestic product by 4 per cent and 5 per cent. Unemployment, however, would fall much less, owing to the rise in productivity – perhaps by 100,000 from fourth quarter to fourth quarter. (The actual fall was about 110,000.) It was thought that the cuts in indirect taxes were sufficient to prevent any rise in retail prices. (The 'all items' retail prices index rose by 0.5 per cent in 1959.) For the moment, fears of inflationary wage increases had been stilled by widespread delays in negotiating the next round. (The actual rise in wages was about 1.25 per cent in 1959.) But there was still no general Government policy, and the third report of the Committee on Prices, Productivity and Incomes, which was published in July, did no more than list possible ways of combating 'the inflationary push which comes when money incomes rise faster than output', without making any recommendations about which, if any, should be used.

Sir Robert Hall, in a note for the Budget Committee at the end of July,[14] concluded that the prospect was for continued moderate growth, and that no present action was needed. The Committee itself, after noting the steep rise in bank advances, showed some uneasiness lest bank credit might became excessive later on, especially in the first quarter of 1960, when a reduced Exchequer surplus would draw off from the market £400 million less than in 1959. But it endorsed the 'no present action' recommendation. Sir Roger Makins, in passing this on to the Chancellor, remarked[15] that

there was little resemblance now with the rapid expansion of 1955. With the single exception of bank advances, all the economic indicators show either less strain on the system, or a stronger economic position than they did in 1955 ... it is quite likely that conditions will remain easy, and the next steps could be slightly more expansionary than the reverse....

This euphoria continued unchallenged almost to the end of 1959. After the Government's election victory in October, 'swan-song' minutes from the outgoing Financial Secretary (Mr J Simon) and Economic Secretary (Mr P J Erroll) took it for granted that there would be some, if not very large, further reduction of taxation in 1960.[16] Sir Edward Boyle, who succeeded as Economic Secretary, while not disputing this, thought it important to strengthen the fiscal weapons for controlling the economy; to that end, he favoured the early introduction of a capital gains tax as a built-in stabiliser which would pay for a raising of the lower limit for surtax, greater and more selective use of investment allowances, and a reform of the Exchequer Accounts to get rid of 'above-the-line' and similar impediments to rational economic budgeting. These ideas drew an appreciative comment from Sir Robert Hall.

The first signs of trouble seem to have been noticed only in December, and then by the Bank of England rather than by the Treasury. The December appraisal of 1959[17] did not differ much from the forecast made after the budget. The growth of final expenditure for the whole year 1959 was put at only 3.5 per cent on 1958, and between the last quarters at only 4.3 per cent. For 1960 as a whole, growth was expected to be faster at about 4.5 per cent but slowing rather than accelerating as the year went on, with the gradual exhaustion of the stimuli given in 1958 and 1959 and the cessation of any rise in the rate of stock building. Retail prices, however, might rise by 1.5 per cent as a result of renewed pressure from rising wage-costs on which the Chancellor had been advised already to give a warning in his Mansion House speech. Sir Robert Hall's report to the Budget Committee, dated 9 December, generally supported the forecasters, and concluded that there was no case for contemplating any change of taxation, up or down, in the 1960 budget. In the Committee, however, there was some dissent.[18] Mr Humphrey Mynors, representing the Bank of England on it for the first time, thought that inflationary developments were likely as a result of a more rapid revival of private investment than was allowed for by the forecast; he was also disturbed by the implications of a Treasury paper on Exchequer finance in 1960: unless the market for gilt-edged could be improved, there would be too many Treasury bills and too big an expansion of the basis for bank credit. The Treasury Overseas Finance side at the same time expressed doubts about the balance of payments. Sir R Makins reported to the Chancellor on 15 December[19] the majority view of the Budget Committee as being, 'provisionally, expansion continuing at a moderate rate, a reasonable balance of payments, and unemployment acceptably low, but not so low as to lead to pressure on resources'; but added that some members thought that the situation might develop in a more inflationary way.

In the New Year the Treasury as well as the Bank became worried about the developing boom, and particularly about the continuing growth of bank advances, which had risen by over one-half since the middle of 1958. At a meeting with the Chancellor on 10 January it was agreed that a 'warning signal' was needed. The Prime Minister, who was abroad, was alerted by cable, and bank rate was raised on 21 January from 4.5 per cent to 5 per cent. At the same time an all round reappraisal was undertaken by the Treasury and the Bank, and it became clear that the brakes must go on again.

Early in 1962 the Economic Section held a post mortem on the reflation of 1958 and 1959 and a year later they tried to apply some of their findings to the management of later stages of the next reflation, in 1963. Their main conclusion was that the measures taken by the Government in 1958 and 1959 had added up to much too much, so that recovery had gone at a pace which could not be sustained and which proved difficult to check in 1960 and 1961. Thus from the third quarter of 1958 to the fourth quarter of 1959 consumers' expenditure rose by £1,060 million at a annual but accelerating rate of 5.6 per cent; fixed investment at 11.7 per cent; and fiscal expenditure at 6.5 per cent, absorbing a rise of £564 million in imports of goods and services. On top of the internal stimuli there was a rise of £600 million in exports, instead of the decline which had been forecast. But the pace of the expansion was only recognised afterwards; and very imperfectly even as late as the NIF reports of December 1959 and February 1960.

The most striking feature was the cumulative and interacting nature of the process. The Economic Section thought that the credit relaxations, which were the first measure, had little immediate effect on expenditure; but, coming after two years of decline in industrial investment, they probably caused some new plans to be made which materialised in orders and expenditure only much later; they also stimulated the demand for private housing. The various doses of public investment which were authorised from July 1958 onwards meant a sharp reversal of the cuts in programmes which had been imposed in September 1957 and caused expenditure to fall for most of 1958. Only in the second quarter of 1959 did public investment recover to the 1957 rate; but once begun, its growth was rapid, and it was fed by further authorisations through 1959, which kept it rising through 1960 and 1961, long after restraints had been reimposed. The first big immediate effect on consumers' spending came from the removal on October 1958 of the severe and long-established restraint on hire purchase. This released (as had, indeed, been expected) a pent-up flood of demand for consumer durables. But, instead of flattening out, as had been forecast, this was reinforced and prolonged by the income tax and other concessions in the 1959 budget, and by the big rise in the money incomes of consumers which went on through 1959 and 1960; this enabled people simultaneously to pay instalments on past hire purchase debt and to incur more of it. Stock-building, very difficult to foresee, also played a big part in the acceleration. The first impact of rising demand was taken by stocks and work-in-progress, and had little effect on production or employment. But it soon reduced the stock ratio to an comfortable level, and so evoked a spate of orders, both for imports and home production, intended both to replace stock already sold and to keep pace with further increases in demand. Information about the movement of stocks and work-in-progress is notoriously unreliable; but, long after the event, the value of their physical increase was stated at £111 million for 1958, £179 million for 1959, and £601 million for 1960. Finally, of course, the unexpected rise in exports had the double effect of both raising incomes, and therefore home demand, and of withdrawing goods originally intended to meet it.

Though the Economic Section's post mortem did not expressly say so, it seems clear from their analysis that the main mistakes made by the Government were, first, to delay too long the removal of hire purchase restrictions or the giving of some equivalent stimulus to consumers' demand; second, to authorise too much public investment, especially after the departmental ceilings were removed altogether in February 1959; third, to remit too much taxation in April 1959, when recovery was already on the way. The Opposition's criticism that the Government should have stimulated industrial investment rather than consumer expenditure does not seem to be justified. An earlier offer of investment allowances, etc., would have had no immediate effect on spending nor, without a rise in demand from consumers, much effect on firms' investment plans. With it, investment allowances in 1958 might have brought these plans forward a little and enlarged them earlier, which would have been helpful. As things went, it is a fair point of criticism that the introduction of investment allowance in April 1959 must have added some fuel to a fire which was already stoked for excessive heat in 1960.

The course of events described above bears little resemblance to the appraisals and forecasts made in the Treasury during the period. The forecasters themselves were certainly aware that serious mistakes were made. Mr Godley, in a minute of 28 December 1962, pointed first to the failure to foresee the rise in exports. This was due to changes in demand in the outside world, not in the British economy, though probably the low level of home demand had something to do with the speed and extent of the response to them. Second, he pointed to the belief that the rate of increase of hire purchase debt would slacken off after the middle of 1959 and so produce a fall in personal consumption; whereas in fact it went on at full tilt until somewhat checked by the reintroduction of controls at the end of April 1960. This mistake was one facet of the general tendency of the forecasts, which Mr Godley did not mention, to underestimate multiplier and momentum effects, both up and down. Third, he thought that the forecasts of personal consumption were too low, even given the assumptions made about exports, investment and public consumption, because the methods used in 1958 were less sophisticated than those used at the end of 1959. He believed, optimistically as it turned out, that these mistakes would not be repeated in future.

My own study of the forecasts suggests that there was a more fundamental trouble: the inability of the forecasters to make a correct appraisal of the level of the economy at the time of the forecast. If this appraisal was too high or too low, it necessarily led to false conclusions about the strain on resources which would be involved in forecast rates of growth, even if these were themselves correct. Striking examples were the failure of the NIF report of December 1958 to record the change of trend in the last quarter of that year, and of that of December 1959 to record the rapid rise in demand and production in the last two quarters of the year and, though the revision in February 1960 picked up some of this, it ignored the further acceleration between the two reports. This weakness was mainly due to the fact that most sources of information then available were wholly inadequate, as for the movement of stocks and industrial investment; badly delayed, as with the index of production; or subject to violent monthly fluctuations, as with imports and exports. The unemployment figures were, indeed, up-to-date and susceptible to fairly accurate seasonal correction. But, as Mr Godley pointed out, unfortunately their movements lagged six months or so behind those of demand and production, as well as having a somewhat variable relation to them. Thus the indicator which was most up-to-date and most in the minds of ministers and officials was sometimes pointing in the wrong direction altogether (unemployment was still rising in February 1959) and at others usually under or over-represented the current pressure of demand and activity. The laymen, however, did not realise the mixed quality of the forecasters' straw, or how much the foundations for their projections had to be influenced by subjective judgement about probabilities rather than by already ascertained figures.

II

The brakes go on again: January 1960 to July 1962

A first necessity was to revise the December forecasts for 1960. Though the new report[20] was only completed on 9 February, its preliminary conclusions were being used a fortnight earlier. The first was that expansion had gone much faster and further in the latter part of 1959 than had been realised in December. Thus, comparing the annual growth between last quarters of 1958 and 1959, consumption was now thought to have risen (at 1954 prices) by £500 million instead of by £270 million, fixed investment by £290 million instead of £230 million; stock building by £300 million against £200 million and, perhaps most important of all, exports by £330 million against £150 million. Overall, the growth of final expenditure at constant prices was now put at 6.5 per cent instead of 4.3 per cent. This meant that the base for further growth in 1960 was much higher, and therefore nearer the level at which capacity and labour resources, especially in the south and the Midlands, would come under strain, with probably inflationary consequences for both wages and prices. It also implied that the momentum for further expansion might be much stronger. But, rather curiously, the authors of the report did not take this second point: their forecasts of growth from the last quarter of 1959 to the last quarter of 1960 were very little higher than in December, apparently because they expected a flattening out of consumption and a fairly early cessation of stock building. (In the event, the first happened, the second did not.)

Most Treasury officials, and the Chancellor, put a more serious gloss on the figures. On 28 January, in a note to the Cabinet[21] covering a paper of his, Sir Robert Hall said that 'the new forecasts indicate a very marked change in the economic outlook', with signs of overstrain already apparent, especially in the building industry. The Chancellor's own reaction was that 'we ought, first, to cut back public investment in 1960/61 in any feasible ways, and, second, have a definitely deflationary budget'. Four days later Sir Frank Lee, the new Permanent Secretary, reported that the Budget Committee now assumed that £100 million of additional taxation ought to be looked for.[22] On 12 February a note[23] prepared for the Prime Minister on his return to England began with three stark points: there was now an inflationary situation, the balance of payments was deteriorating because of a great rise in imports, and stable prices were not likely to last much longer. For 1960, the prospective rise of 4 per cent or more in demand on domestic resources and of 5 per cent in imports 'would produce an intolerably tight labour position, and another autumn crisis for the pound could not be ruled out'. Therefore, a general tightening up was required, and, particularly, a very critical look at all proposals for more expenditure by Government, local authorities, and nationalised industries.

This sudden swing of official opinion from complacency as late as September, through mild disquiet in December, to a tone of near-panic in February, is very remarkable. There was a sense that they had been caught napping. The Chancellor, who had muttered caution several times before and since the budget, needed little urging, and nor did the Secretary (Sir Edward Boyle); but a note[24] which the latter prepared for the Chancellor's use, in discussions with the Prime Minister shows that they had much trouble with him and with some of their colleagues. This note emphasised that we could not afford a risk with the balance of payments; that it was better to curb consumption than investment, using both budgetary and monetary means; and that if action were taken at once it would still be possible to have a continuing rise in the standard of living, with perhaps 3 per cent growth in output. But if things were left to slide and there were another balance of payments crisis in the autumn, very drastic measures would be needed.

Outside opinion was also not ready for a quick change of front. The Trade Union Congress, in their pre-budget representations, reproached the Chancellor for allowing a rise in bank-rate when there were still 400,000 unemployed, and demanded further measures to raise demand and so to take back into employment labour which was being displaced by rising productivity, and in the development districts. The Federation of British Industry thought that no extraordinary stimulus was needed, but asked for the conversion of the remaining initial allowances into investment allowances, and for reductions in surtax and income tax. The Conservative Research Department recommended that, if any restraint were necessary monetary rather than budgetary instruments should be used. The Conservative Finance Committee, headed by Mr Enoch Powell, said that 'preservation of monetary stability should have first and over-riding priority', but added that there would be grave disappointment if there were not some further remissions, particularly of death duties and surtax, during the first half of the new Parliament. But not even they seriously pressed for cuts in Government expenditure, although the estimates for 1960/61 were £353 million – nearly 7 per cent – above those for 1959/60.

The Chancellor's task was not made easier presentationally by the unexpected buoyancy of the revenue. Total tax receipts for 1959/60 turned out to be £290 million (5.7 per cent) above the budget estimate,** the surplus above the line £386 million instead of £102 million, and the overall deficit £314 million instead of £721 million. For 1960/61, despite the rise in expenditure, the above the line surplus was estimated at £372 million before tax changes. Narrowly budgetary arithmetic would therefore have to be based on the need to cover more of the below-the-line, mainly capital, expenditure, by taxation. But, even in inflationary circumstances a move actually to raise taxation for that purpose would be very unpopular in the House.

---

*   The Inland Revenue were the worst offenders on this occasion, and were made to look very foolish in the Budget Committee; but expenditure below-the-line had also been overestimated by the Treasury. Large differences between estimates and out-turn of the overall deficit had been a feature of the past decade. The overestimate of £407 million for 1959/60 was the largest yet, but it had been around £300 million in three of the years, and there had been an underestimate of £361 million in 1952/53. The differences were often much larger than the planned budget changes, which they sometimes offset, sometimes exaggerated.

After the alarms of February, there seems to have been some reaction. A note to the Chancellor on 1 March laid great stress on the worsening balance of payments and on the need now to 'exercise a mild check on expansionist forces at home', but did not attempt to quantify this. The Economic Section reported on 2 March that expansion was continuing without signs of slackening, but emphasised that the re-stocking boom could not go on indefinitely, and pointed out that wages were as yet only 1.3 per cent above the level of January 1959, though plenty of increases were in the pipeline. The Chancellor had by then decided that in the political circumstances he could not make drastic use of the budgetary weapon. The brave talk of a definitely deflationary budget and £100 million of new taxation came to very little. In the budget introduced on 4 April Profits Tax was raised from 10 per cent to 12.5 per cent. This might have some psychological effect, but would not draw its full annual yield of £65 million until 1961/62 and later. Tobacco duty was increased, to yield £29 million more with immediate impact; but this was offset by minor concessions of income tax and estate duty, and by the repeal of the entertainments tax on cinemas and television shows. In its effect on 1960/61 it was almost a 'neutral' budget. The Chancellor did, however, give clear warning of further restriction of credit:

Last year we were glad to see an expansion of credit, and it made a notable contribution to stimulating the economy. Now, I judge that we must be cautious. First steps in changing the climate for private lending have already been taken by the change in bank rate in January and by open-market transactions ... I think it likely that the time may soon arrive when we should take other steps to restrain the expansion of private credit; and we stand ready to do so.[25]

The budget did, however, provide for a surplus above the line of £304 million and an overall deficit of only £318 million. These aims for 1960/61 were close to the actual outturn for 1959/60, but of course much less expansionary than its original plan.

Parliamentary criticism was limited. For the Opposition, Mr Gaitskell and Mr Wilson confined themselves mainly to taunts about a 'morning after budget', though Mr Roy Jenkins developed the theme that the main trouble was low investment, with slow growth of productivity and a deteriorating balance of payments as the result; he thought that the great failure of 1958 and 1959 had been that the Government initiated a consumer boom first, instead of stimulating investment first by earlier and more generous tax allowances. Mr Nabarro attacked the increases in taxation as 'an act of political turpitude' and, with 12 other Conservatives, abstained on the budget resolution. Mr Thorneycroft rammed home the fact that, after less than two years of expansion, we had reached a position where taxes should be raised and credit drastically tightened. Why? He thought that the main cause was the 'inevitably inflationary' effect of the steep rise in public expenditure, and that there ought to be more frank speaking both about its future prospects and about the means for financing it.

The credit measures foreshadowed by the Chancellor were in fact already largely planned, and were applied within the month. Hire purchase restrictions were reimposed by the Board of Trade, in the form, generally, of a requirement of a minimum deposit of 20 per cent and a maximum period of two years for repayment. These conditions were much less rigorous than those which had applied from 1956 to 1958; they were, indeed, probably not much more rigorous than the terms offered commercially by most of the reputable hire purchase finance companies. But their imposition may have had some psychological effect on would-be hire purchasers, and served also somewhat to placate the joint stock banks, whose competing personal loans scheme would certainly have to be cut back as part of the simultaneous attempt to limit their advances. The Treasury and the Bank considered, but rejected as both unnecessary and impracticable, plans for imposing ceilings on lending by the finance companies and other non-banking lenders.[26] To the banks themselves the Bank of England applied the new instrument of a call for special deposits, which had been negotiated with them as a reserve when the advances ceilings and directives were removed in the summer of 1958. On 28 April it required the London Clearing Banks to deposit with it sums equal to 1 per cent of their own total deposits; for the Scottish banks the requirement was 0.5 per cent. This in effect froze some £75 million of the banks' resources and reduced the total money supply by the same amount. On 23 June the Bank made a second call of the same amount, and bank rate was raised from 5 per cent to 6 per cent, mainly to relieve the strain on sterling.

The need for drastic monetary action had of course been increased by the weakness of the budget. But there was a strong case for it in its own right. It was impossible to deny that the rise of bank advances by nearly a half – over £800 million – since 1958 had stimulated the boom both in investment and in consumer spending: £300 of the increase was in the 'Personal and Professional' category. It had also been the main vehicle, because loans create deposits, for an increase of a similar amount (though a much smaller proportion, about 9 per cent) in the total money supply. But, as the Bank frequently pointed out, the problem of control was complicated by the needs of Exchequer financing, both for the current deficit and for maturing debt. If the Government increased its sales of Treasury bills, it directly increased the liquid assets of the banks and thus made possible, within the banks' conventional 30 per cent ratio of liquid assets to deposits, a more than threefold increase in the money supply. But it could only carry through the traditional policy of funding as much debt as possible if the general public's confidence in gilt-edged were maintained by keeping up their price. When, therefore, as throughout 1959, the clearing banks offered securities for sale in order to expand their advances, the Bank felt obliged to buy them; and this increased the liquid assets of the clearing bank, by another route. The new special deposits requirement was in effect a means of temporarily sterilising the increase in the money supply which the Government's own policy had created. But the banks could, for some time at least, offset the requirement and keep up the expansion of their (higher yielding) advances by continuing to offer gilt-edged securities for the Government to buy; and then another tranche of special deposit requirements might become necessary, as actually happened in July 1961. Special deposits were useful in imposing a check and in gaining time, but were not in themselves a cure so long as demand remained strong and the credit ratings of borrowers high. Advances were, after all, the most profitable part of the business of the clearing banks.

The June NIF report[27] covered the period to the middle of 1961, and was even more than usually difficult to interpret because of the differences between its expectations when expressed in money terms and in real terms. It began by forecasting that the wage and salary bill would be more than 6 per cent higher than in the first half of 1960, and total personal income 5 per cent higher; but that, owing to the rise in retail prices, consumers' spending in real terms would rise by only 2.5 per cent, and the gross domestic product by the same amount. It thought that the demand for investment goods would rise by 10 per cent , but actual expenditure by not more than 7 per cent, because of supply difficulties, especially in the building industry. It accepted a forecast from the Balance of Payments Working Party of 'a marked fall' in the growth of exports, to under 3 per cent above the first half of 1960. It did not think that pressure on resources would increase much further; unemployment, seasonally adjusted, was likely to remain about constant over the period.

An Economic Section note[28] about the same date, however, stressed the continuing rise in employment and in bank advances, despite the budget and the credit restrictions, and concluded that .the pressure of demand was still rising dangerously. The Bank of England took the same view and, as has been said, a second round of credit measures was applied on 23 June. But the forecasts probably contributed to an apparently general belief that the boom would soon moderate and that the restrictions need not last long. The Chancellor thought it timely to give the Cabinet in early July a paper on the forecast Estimates for 1961/62, in which he pointed out that supply expenditure was still likely to grow much faster than the gross national product, and concluding 'if we let this happen, we give up hope of lower taxation'.[29] In the House on 11 July he said that the aim was simply to moderate expansion: the economy was generally in good shape, but export performance was not good enough and rising money incomes were pushing up costs and prices. He stated again that the aims of economic policy were to safeguard the pound and to maintain price stability. This was Mr Heathcoat Amory's last major speech before he was succeeded by Mr Selwyn Lloyd as Chancellor on 27 July 1960.

Mr Selwyn Lloyd's appointment did not mark any changes of policy or method in the control of demand. The papers suggest that his main interests were elsewhere.[30] He wished above all to secure radical simplifications in the tax system, and to carry much further the shift from direct to indirect taxation, which had already gone some way. It was his misfortune that the economic circumstances did not leave room for radical changes in 1961 and 1962. He did, however, accept, and came to welcome, plans to take powers to use a fiscal 'economic regulator' outside the budget, and this was in fact the main feature of his first Finance Bill. As time went on he became absorbed in the attempt to develop direct means of checking the rise of wages the 'pause' and the 'guiding light'; but there is no sign that the precise relationship of this to the older policy of control of demand was clearly thought out and established, and the responsibilities for it in the Treasury were mostly in different hands.

By September it seemed that the restriction of credit was beginning to bite. At a meeting with the Chancellor on 13 September[34] there was agreement that the economy had begun to level out in July, and the impact of the credit restrictions was expected to become progressive for the rest of the year. The bank rate had already attracted a big influx of foreign funds. This did, indeed, become so big that bank rate had to be reduced to 5.5 per cent on 27 October and to 5 per cent on 8 December, without much regard to the internal situation. But it did appear, by November, that the growth both of hire purchase debt and of bank advances had been sharply checked.

The underlying position was, however, far from good. Though both retail sales. (by volume) and industrial production had fallen since the middle of the year, pressure on the labour market appeared to have increased, at least in the south and Midlands; unemployment, seasonally adjusted, had gone on falling. Retail prices continued to rise, and each new wage settlement was higher than the one before. Imports were still soaring, while exports had been falling since the spring (though they recovered in the last quarter). Finally, there was anxiety about a recession in the United States, and about the weakness of the dollar which, it was thought, largely accounted for the temporary strengthening of the pound. The medicine recommended to the Chancellor and his colleagues in November was the same as before: continued restraints until the balance of payments improves, possibly a tough budget in 1961, with a question whether anything could be done to improve efficiency and increase exports?[32]

The December forecast for 1961[33] was equally gloomy. The rise in gross domestic product and industrial production would be very small, around 1 per cent; since this was probably less than the growth of productivity, unemployment would rise by about 80,000. Wage rates would be 6 per cent higher in June 1961 than a year earlier, and retail prices would rise by 2.5 per cent per annum. The one bright spot was that private investment was expected to go on rising, though more slowly; but it was thought that a cessation of stock building would offset most of the effects of this on demand. The February revision[34] of this forecast was more hopeful, expecting a bigger growth in consumer spending because of wage increases and the minor relaxations of hire purchase controls which had been made in January; rather higher manufacturing investment; and, in a further revision made in March[35], better exports: in all, bringing the growth of domestic product nearer to 2.5 per cent in real terms. But wages and prices were expected to go up even faster than before.

Both Sir Robert Hall and Sir Frank Lee took a poor view of these forecasts.[36] Though the rate expansion indicated was small, they thought that neither the wage/price position nor the balance of payments left room for any stimulation of demand. They also thought that credit had taken too much of the burden of control so far. They therefore suggested, tentatively in December, definitely in February, either a 'standstill' budget or some increase in taxation to allow for a let-up in credit restrictions; and the Budget Committee on 13 February formally advised that additional taxation of at least £100 million net was necessary. As Sir Robert Hall put it, 'with the overall balance of payments strongly in deficit throughout 1960 and not much improvement in prospect: for 1961, the only solution is an expansion of exports; and this requires restraint of home demand'. The

Chancellor, however, showed in discussions on 3 and 27 February[37] much aversion to a tough budget, and still insisted upon reductions, particularly in surtax, in order to produce 'an incentives budget'. He argued that much of any remission of surtax would be saved, and that it would not, in any case, increase purchasing power before January 1962. It was only under strong official pressure that to offset this he agreed to a further increase in Profits Tax, from 12.5 per cent to 15 per cent, whose effects would also be delayed, and to increases in petrol and motor vehicle duties, which would add about £60 million to taxation. There was another formal submission on 15 March[38] that at least £100 million was needed, but the Chancellor refused to agree to this.

The probable weakness in the budget itself increased the importance of the proposals for an extra-budgetary economic regulator, to which the Chancellor had been sympathetic but not finally committed. It now appealed to him as a useful insurance, since, if the necessary powers were taken in the Finance Act, and if it were clearly needed, it would enable him to impose extra taxation after the budget. But not much time was left.

Work on the possibilities of an economic regulator had been started by the Budget Committee on 16 June 1960. The basic need was to find some form of tax, with wide incidence and substantial yield, which could be imposed or remitted at any time and with immediate impact on consumers' spending. A quickly variable general sales tax or food tax was to be examined; the possibility of making changes in profits tax bite more quickly was mentioned; and the Economic Section were asked to produce a paper on wages and pay-roll taxes, which was circulated on 22 July.[39] The 'regulator' idea was mentioned to the new Chancellor on 12 September, and he agreed, without much enthusiasm, that work should proceed. On 19 October Customs and Excise, apparently on their own initiative, outlined a theme for a flat surcharge or deduction applicable to all Customs and Excise duties; they calculated that 5 per cent plus or minus would give a range of variation of £240 million in a year.

On 26 October the Budget Committee gave a session to discussion of the possibilities concentrating on the Customs' proposal and on various forms of pay-roll tax, as alternatives. Most members preferred the former, because it was simple, would use existing machinery, would not affect export prices, and could perhaps be more easily reserved for anti-cyclical use than a pay-roll tax, which was at that time being advocated elsewhere as a means of encouraging economy in the use of labour or checking the growth of employment in congested parts of the country. A submission to the Chancellor on 8 November[40] put the case as follows:

1. The need for a further instrument of cyclical control 'to supplement or replace the existing ones' was widely recognised.
2. Such a tax should particularly affect consumption, and should act quickly and widely.
3. If possible, it should be enacted in such a way that it could be introduced, varied, or remitted otherwise than in the budget, e.g. by Treasury Order.
4 It should in principle be reserved for cyclical use. There was, however, no constitutional way of ensuring that it could not be imposed as an alternative to raising other taxes; or, that, when reflation was needed, reductions in it should have precedence over reductions of other taxes.

5. Of various proposals, a General Sales Tax, already examined in 1957, would be cumbersome to collect and politically difficult because it must cover food. A cumulative Turnover Tax would be too complicated for frequent variation. A wages or pay-roll tax was practicable, and suitable for the aim. But it would be politically difficult, and it could not according to the Inland Revenue, be collected through the existing PAYE income tax machinery. A variant, to collect it by varying up or down the National Insurance contributions paid by employers, by workers or by both, would be practicable; but it would threaten the actuarial justification for contributions, which both Treasury and the Ministry of Pensions and National Insurance thought it essential to preserve. Moreover, if, to avoid political trouble, employers' contributions alone were varied, the effect on prices and spending would be wholly indirect, and slow; export costs would also be affected.
6. Therefore a special surcharge/rebate on all existing Customs and Excise Duties and on Purchase Tax was recommended as the best hope.

This recommendation was repeated in a further submission on 1 January 1961,[41] which also explained why the coverage could not readily be widened to include vehicle and television licence duties, which were mainly collected for a year at a time. The Chancellor himself, however, early in January, perhaps influenced by a talk with Lord Robbins, Lord Plowden and Sir A Spearman,[42] suggested more examination of the possibility of varying employers' National Insurance contributions, and this found a strong protagonist within the Treasury in Sir Thomas Padmore (then Second Secretary). After much heated discussion with MPNI a plan was evolved for a flat-rate addition of up to 2s a week (later raised to 4s) to the employers' contributions alone. This would be imposed by Treasury Order, and collected on the same stamps as the ordinary contribution, but paid into the Exchequer instead of into the National Insurance Fund. At 4s, without exemptions or discriminations, it would draw off money from employers at the rate of about £190 million a year. Most of this would be passed on in increased prices; in so far as it was not, net profits would be reduced, but by a smaller amount because the charge would be a cost like any other for the computation of taxable profits. The plan did not provide for any abatement of ordinary contributions when reflation was needed: it was thus, unlike the Customs and Excise regulator, one way only. It would, indeed, have been perfectly possible to provide for payments from the Exchequer to the National Insurance Fund to finance appropriate reductions of the stamps. But it was objected that this would set a dangerous precedent for subsidising the Fund for other reasons – a disingenuous relic of the earlier objection to using the contributions as a vehicle at all.

The joint Treasury and MPNI paper[46] summed up on the whole against the plan. It added to previous objections the fact that, since eight to 12 weeks would be required for the printing and distribution of new stamps, a surcharge could not be very quick acting; and it emphasised that such a surcharge must expose a politically dangerous flank to plausible demands for differential rates and exemptions which would, if granted, undermine its effect and complicate its administration. But the inadequacy of the main budget proposals caused Sir Frank Lee and Sir Thomas Padmore to advise the Chancellor to seek powers for both the Customs and Excise surcharge and the insurance surcharge; and in early March he accepted this with some enthusiasm. The Minister of Pensions appealed to the Cabinet against the insurance surcharge and there was some further vain examination of a separate poll-tax as an alternative, before the Chancellor got his way.

The Chancellor announced both 'regulators' as a main feature of his budget speech on 17 April, and sought powers in the Finance Bill to use them at any time by Treasury Order. Constitutional objections were met by providing that the powers would lapse in August 1962, unless they had been renewed by the Ways and Means Resolution and Finance Act of that year; and also by providing that any Statutory Order made under them would lapse unless it was confirmed by affirmative resolution of the House within 21 days. The Customs regulator was 'all or nothing': any surcharge, or rebate, must apply to all the specified duties at a uniform rate, not exceeding 10 per cent. The insurance surcharge, up to 4s a week, on the other hand, could be used with differential rates, or with exemptions, for different classes of persons. Neither, of course, could be used until the Finance Bill became law about the middle of July.

The Customs regulator was generally approved both inside and outside the House, but the insurance regulator met great hostility. This was largely grounded on the idea that it was wrong to tax employment, especially in development areas or of the disabled, women, part-time workers, etc. But this regulator was also attacked by those who wanted a permanent pay-roll tax to encourage economy in the use of labour. The Chancellor himself muddled the issues by adducing this as a secondary reason for introducing it as a regulator. The insurance clause was debated for over seven hours on 13 June. The effect on the Chancellor was considerable. He refused to use this regulator as part of his July measures, and he dropped the power to use it from the next Finance Bill. The contributions surcharge was killed by lack of clear thinking about what its objects really were, and its advantages as a regulator, if coupled with a rebate as well, were neither squarely looked at nor tested in practice.

The main feature of the budget itself was the introduction of earnings allowance and earned income relief for surtax payers, at a delayed cost of over £80 million, offset, as has been said, by an increase in Profits Tax whose yield was also deferred. It was argued that the combination would give a spur to individual efficiency while discouraging over-expansion by companies; but this seems highly doubtful. The immediate increases in the duties on oil, motor vehicles and television advertisements were expected to yield about £80 million, too narrowly based to have much general effect on spending. But they did raise the estimated above the line surplus for 1961/62 to £506 million, leaving an overall deficit of £69 million only. This much relieved the difficulties of Exchequer financing and of the control of bank credit. The Opposition alleged that the increases in the rates of National Insurance contributions and benefits, which had been announced by the Minister of Health in January, also represented a stiff dose of deflation. Calculations inside the Treasury threw doubt on this. It was true that at the new rates contribution (leaving aside the Exchequer supplement) were expected to increase in 1961/62 by about £74 million more than benefits, instead of £20 million less in 1960/61.[44] But, because of the difference in circumstances between beneficiaries and contributors 'an extra pound paid in benefits has so much more effect in increasing spending than an extra taken in contributions has in reducing it, that the net effect will be almost nil'. The general Economic Section judgement was that this was not a tough budget; after allowing for multiplier and savings effects together, the total measure of restraint could not be put at more than £80 million to £100 million over the year – about one-third of 1 per cent of total domestic expenditure at current prices.

The budget did nothing to steady the economy, or to relieve the growing doubts about the balance of payments. Before the end of May the Bank of England were pointing to a big fall in the reserves and were asking the Treasury for effective action; and Sir Denis Rickett (Second Secretary on the Finance side) minuted that 'he would strongly support the use of one or both of the regulators as soon as available.'[45] The June NIF report[46] (dated 1 June, but largely drafted a month earlier) expected a much more rapid expansion of demand than had been forecast in February and more than double that in December. In an interesting discussion of the pressure on resources which this implied, the authors put the growth of productive capacity between the second halves of 1961 and 1962 at 2.75/3.5 per cent for the gross domestic product and at 3/4 per cent for industrial production, after allowing for an above average growth of the working population, due to the post-war bulge in births and to immigration, and also for the maturing of unusually large additions to industrial capital. Thus the forecast increase of 3.8 per cent in domestic product and 4.5/5 per cent in industrial production could only be achieved by a clear further rise in the use of capacity. But pressure was already very high, with unemployment down to 1.3 per cent in May. If, in addition, exports were to rise by 5 per cent, as required for the balance of payments, instead of the modest 1 per cent forecast, pressure on resources 'would reach a point not far short of the highest levels reached since the war', with effects on wages and prices which it was not easy to judge.

Mr Alec Cairncross, who had just succeeded Sir Robert Hall as Economic Adviser, put this view to the Budget Committee on 6 June,[47] adding the rider that, with three successive years of deficit on current account in the balance of payments, it was vital to make room for a big expansion of commodity exports. He thought that a reduction in domestic purchasing power at the rate of £600 million a year would be needed both to free resources for exports and to prevent further pressure on demand; but he suggested as a first step a cut of £300 million, which would still allow total output to rise at the same rate as industrial capacity. The Committee decided to recommend the Chancellor to put in the first line the use of both regulators as soon as the Finance Bill became law at the end of July – Customs surcharge at the full 10 per cent, and the contributions surcharge at 2s a week at least, which together would draw off spending power at the rate of about £300 million a year. But the exchange position had to be held in the meantime and a broader 'package' prepared which would contain longer-term remedies as well; confidence in the pound at home and abroad could not be restored simply by the medicine as before. All this was discussed with a startled Chancellor at meetings on 6 and 15 June, at which the Governor was present, as well as the junior Treasury ministers, Mr Barber and Sir Edward Boyle.[48]

Outside the Treasury and the Bank, though the signs of an incipient balance of payments crisis were obvious, there seems to have been a willingness to accept either that the economy was overstrained or that a general restoration of demand would help the balance of payments. An analysis by the Economic Section of articles in the *Economist*, *Guardian*, *Observer* and *Financial Times* showed something like a consensus that only select remedies were needed – direct restraint of excessive wage increases, more industrial investment 'to improve flexibility', a damping of demand on those industries where excessive demand was pulling prices up, combined with more demand on others when prices are pushed up by the high costs of working below capacity. These pundits did not indicate, however, how Government could apply these remedies. The TUC, at a meeting with the Chancellor on 15 June, made their usual plea for more expansion, accompanied if necessary by the use of selective controls such as building licensing. Even in early July Sir Norman Kipping and Mr Hugh Weeks, representing the FBI, advocated expanding production, relying on a growth of exports which they predicted, and eschewing deflation; they thought that a 'shock' resistance to wage increases and a drive for cost reduction and competitiveness offered the best hope for the balance of payments. Even among ministers, the Prime Minister and others for some time thought that a further dose of credit restrictions and perhaps the use of credit controls would be right and sufficient: the negotiation of an effective 'package', affecting many departments, therefore proved very difficult.

The Governor early reported that at a meeting with other central banks at Basle he had secured offers of help up to £250 million. This would perhaps be enough to see us through June and July, but it was a short-term facility only. He asked and received authority to draw a gold tranche of £190 million from the International Monetary Fund, and also one, or even two, credit tranches of US$500 million each. But he was sure that money would not flow back to London unless much wider corrective action were taken; indeed, we should have to show this in order to obtain credit tranches from the Fund. We did not in fact ask the IMF for these until such action had been taken on 25 July. In the Treasury, Mr R W B Clarke made a strong case for a drastic attack on public expenditure:[49] a pause for six months in the authorisation of all Government and local authority starts in building and civil engineering and, for the longer run, major changes of policy for spending on defence and education and cuts in the subsidies to agriculture and industry; and Government expenditure overseas must be reduced. But specific decisions could not be obtained at once; for instance, Sir Norman Brook, in a report to the Prime Minister,[50] said that a reduction of overseas military expenditure from £235 million to £200 million could only be achieved by withdrawing altogether from some theatres, and ministers were not ready for such difficult choices. Yet without precise decisions the undertaking which the Chancellor gave to keep the growth of supply expenditure in 1962/63 within 2.5 per cent in real terms looked vain, and was later proved to be so. The Government did indeed at last adopt a positive stand on wage increases, and plunged for the 'pause': an appeal, which the public sector would exemplify, for a total cessation of increases for about nine months, to allow time for productivity to catch up and for a longer term formula to be worked out.

It also decided to set up a new consultative body with both sides of industry – the National Economic Development Council as it was later called – which it was hoped would co-ordinate forward planning, help to work out a general wages policy, and suggest means of improving industrial efficiency competitiveness. There were also to be more credit restrictions: a third call on the clearing banks for special deposits, directives to them to reduce especially advances for consumption purposes and for property speculation, and the raising of bank rate from 5 per cent to 7 per cent. Control was also to be tightened on private investment overseas and on the remittance of overseas profits to the UK. But because of opposition from the Board of Trade, the partial relaxation of hire purchase controls which had been made in January was not reversed. Finally, on the fiscal side, while agreeing to apply the Customs regulator at 10 per cent, the Chancellor steadily refused to make any use of the contributions regulator, (the 'dead rat', as he called it) even though the Financial Secretary pressed him to do so in order to make an impact abroad.[51] Sir Thomas Padmore tried to force his hand by advising as a necessary substitute an increase of 6*d* in income tax and a suspension of the budget concessions on surtax,[52] but without effect.

These 'July measures' were announced by the Chancellor to the House on 2 July in a speech which both in substance and in tone fell far short of Treasury advice and drafts, though they probably removed more domestic purchasing power than Mr Cairncross's 'first step' of £300 million, which he had recommended early in June. Since then his view had become gloomier. In a very simplified calculation on the 18 July,[53] dealing with the change from the first half of 1961 to the first half of 1962, he stated the 'permissible' increase in gross domestic product at £450 million, of which £350 million was needed to improve the foreign balance, either by more exports or less imports; only £100 million ought therefore to go to the home market. But final domestic demand, before the July measures, was expected to grow by £1,150 million.* Even if the measures removed £700 million, which he greatly doubted, there would still be about £300 million too much. Either the necessary improvement in the foreign balance would not take place, or the economy would become still more over-strained, with the usual further inflation of wages and prices. In retrospect, this much exaggerated the reduction needed to overcome the strain, and was much too optimistic about the growth of exports in 1962. On the other hand, Mr R W B Clarke, writing the brief for the meeting with the International Monetary Fund,[57] seems now too optimistic about public expenditure:

the key point, for sophisticated observers, is the Government's intention to take a grip on public expenditure. Long-term actions are more important than short, for the latter would be regarded as the mixture as before, to be discarded as soon as the immediate crisis is past ...

---

*   These figures were, in principle, at 1954 prices. At current 1961/62 prices they would be
      15-20 per cent more. But the '£350 million needed to improve the foreign balance' seems to
      have been taken from a 'current price' calculation, and was therefore some £30 million too
      high in relation to the other figures.

In the short term, these July measures seemed very successful. They removed fears of early devaluation, which had contributed more to the exchange crisis than the balance of payments deficit itself. The strain on the pound eased at once, with a big return of funds, so that after some delay and controversy base rate was reduced to 6.5 per cent on 6 October, and then progressively to 4.5 per cent by 26 April 1962. Imports fell sharply in the last half of 1961, and the current account for the year was practically in balance with an actual credit on the capital account. The economy also flattened out. The volume of retail sales became fairly steady, though prices went on rising. Industrial production actually fell until the end of the year and total unemployment rose substantially above its low point of 293,000 (United Kingdom) in July. The pressure on resources was certainly relieved in the short term. But the longer-term measures were mostly failures, as was already becoming evident, when in March 1962 a post mortem was made at the Chancellor's request.[55] The NEDC was indeed set up, with a permanent staff headed by Sir Robert Shone; but the TUC refused to give it much help, and its contribution to either the efficiency or the manageability of the economy is debatable. It probably complicated the Government's task by its consistently expansionist pressures. The 'wage pause' lasted until the end of March 1962, and was followed by a 'guiding light' for increases not normally to exceed 2.5 per cent a year. It had some partial success at first. Hourly wage rates had been rising at the rate of 6 per cent to 7 per cent a year from the last quarter of 1960 to the middle of 1961. After a short lag due to claims in the pipe-line, it dropped to 4 per cent by the end of the year, and stayed between 4 per cent and 5 per cent throughout 1962. But the rate of increase still much exceeded the growth of average productivity and it again accelerated in 1963 and 1964. There was no real 'pause' and after the 'guiding light', as had been feared, guided to minimum rather than to maximum or average increases, failure to hold public expenditure was even sooner evident. Though some check was authorised on fresh additions to the investment programme, particularly of local authorities, the supply estimates for 1962/63 showed a rise of about 6 per cent* in money terms, against the 2.5 per cent which the Chancellor had stated as the limit. None of the major decisions needed to contain yet further increases were taken in July, and after the recess the heat was off.

The aim of keeping Government expenditure overseas in 1962 within £200 million was, indeed, just achieved; but it rose steeply again later. The promised tightening of control over outward investment came to little. This was perhaps fortunate, since interest, profits and dividends from overseas, which had been stable from 1955 to 1961, rose from £674 million in 1961 to £900 million in 1965 – one of the brighter spots in our balance of payments.

It is not easy to justify the official Treasury handling of the July crisis. It is clear in retrospect that they overestimated the amount of deflation needed to deal with it in the

---

*   Most of this was the result of decisions taken much earlier. Even had they been reversed, it
     is most unlikely that expenditure in 1961–63 could have been reduced to the target. Most
     of the savings would have materialised only later.

short term. The fiscal and credit measures taken, though less than officials recommended, proved ample to stop the immediate troubles of the pound, and caused a short-term fall in production which was greater than officials either predicted or desired. But in fairness it must be said that they had their eyes as much on 1962 as on 1961, and wanted to free resources then for a much faster growth of exports. In the event, exports did rise substantially in the first half of 1962, and excessive pressure of demand seemed to be developing again, until it was relieved by a fall in industrial investment and a rise in unemployment in the autumn of 1962. If the advice of officials had been more fully taken in July 1961, this general recession would probably have come earlier, and it might have been accompanied by a bigger check to the rise of wage costs and an earlier shake-out of redundant labour. In that case, however, the reversal of the policy of restraint would, given the climate of opinion, probably also have come earlier and with greater contrast. There seems to be no basis for guessing whether this would have left the economy in better or worse shape in the years ahead.

By the autumn it was clear that the economy had steadied down. The question was whether it would stay so, without either a deepening recession or renewed pressure on resources. The November forecast[56] suggested that it would. The authors expected the gross domestic product to recover fairly sharply in the first half of 1962, but with then only a slow rise in the second half and early in 1963. There would be a rise of 9 per cent in exports in 1962 but, on the basis of the latest replies to the Board of Trade from industrialists, a large fall in manufacturing investment; this would, however, be about offset by the of growth of other investment, public and private. Expansion on this scale would be consistent with unemployment averaging about 1.8 per cent – 450,000. It should not involve any particular strain on real resources, though both wages and prices would go on rising. Mr Cairncross, expounding this to the Budget Committee,[57] said that there was no danger of a deepening recession, and little, if any, room for fiscal or other relaxations. Mr William Armstrong pointed out that two of the assumptions of the forecast – that public expenditure would be held within the limit set in July, and that the next round of wage increases would not exceed 3.5 per cent were not likely to be realised; and he also pointed to the fall in the latest estimates of the Inland Revenue for tax receipts for 1962/63. Sir Frank Lee, reporting the discussion to the Chancellor,[58] emphasised the need for at least a 'no change' budget (with the Customs regulator or an equivalent still applied), and warned that a net increase in taxation might be needed, either to deal with the economy, or to cover an excess of supply expenditure above the undertaking of July, or to make room for relaxations of the credit squeeze in order to help industrial investment. This contrasted strongly with the view developed by the Economist early in January, that there should be an expansionary budget to lift demand, but accompanied by the maintenance of high interest rates and a tough wages policy.

The February forecast[59] recognised that the fall both in demand and production late in 1961 had gone further than had been thought in November, and that the starting point for 1962 was therefore lower; but it was thought that the expansionary forces – public expenditure and rising wage incomes – would be stronger and manufacturing investment at least no worse, so that the rate of growth of domestic product would be faster, at about 5 per cent over the year, and to a slightly higher level in the first quarter of 1963. Much of the forecast increase was, however, accounted for by an assumed substitution of home production for imports and by the expected rise of in exports. Mr Cairncross' conclusion was the same as in November; 'we should probably recommend a neutral budget'. The Bank and the finance side were troubled about the borrowing requirement to cover the rising public expenditure, both actual and prospective, and Sir Richard Powell (Board of Trade) thought that the forecast growth of home demand might hold back exports. The Committee therefore recommended that the budget should have a slight tilt towards restraint and that, if the Chancellor thought that the economy needed some stimulus, he should relax credit rather than reduce taxes. Sir Frank Lee covered this recommendation on 23 February with the advice[60] that 'given expansionary forces in the economy, leading to an even higher level of activity in 1963 than previously forecast, the unmistakable need will be for a policy of continued restraint'. At about the same time Lord Cromer, who had been Economic Minister in Washington, commenting to the Chancellor[61] on rumours current in the United States and elsewhere that HMG intended to devalue sterling if and when we joined the Common Market, wrote: 'the position of the Exchequer this year or next may well lead them to think that this will not be a matter of choice.'

The Chancellor, though clearly unhappy with this advice, did not seriously dispute it. He agreed to the incorporation in ordinary taxation of the regulator surcharge: this, though 'no change' as compared with the present, meant an increase of some £200 million in indirect taxes compared with the last budget. He agreed also to renew his power to use the Customs regulator, but stressed in his budget speech that this use could be downward as well as upward. After various minor changes, however, there was no 'tilt': the net result shown in the Financial Statement on 9 April was a reduction of taxation by £9.5 million in 1962/63, but an increase of £9 million in a full year. The overall deficit (or budget borrowing requirement) for 1962/63 was estimated at £74 million: in 1961/62 because of heavy supplementary estimates, it had turned out to be £211 million instead of the £69 million originally provided for. The Cabinet, as well as the House, were clearly disappointed, and were probably not convinced by the economic diagnosis. Two days later the Prime Minister wrote to the Chancellor:[62]

We ought to be preparing straight away possibilities for next year on the assumption that the economic situation will allow an expansionist budget and a substantial reduction of taxation. Do not leave it too late.

The policy of restraint was obviously wearing thin, whatever its merits might be and these were increasingly disputed by those who argued that rapid growth offered the only hope of reducing costs and absorbing irresistible wage increases. Bank rate came down to 4.5 per cent on 26 April; on 31 May the Bank reduced its call for special deposits from 3 per cent to 2 per cent; and on 4 June the minimum deposit for hire purchase was reduced from 20 per cent to 10 per cent for all goods except cars – a move which had been rejected as premature in April. The summer fall in unemployment was less than usual, and the figure for June, 432,000 in the United Kingdom, was nearly half as big again as a year earlier, though still only 1.8 per cent. Disquiet grew among the public and in Parliament, and there was a widespread view that a reflation of demand was needed to stop a recession, quite apart from stimulating growth. This came especially from industry, where many firms were conscious of a tapering off of their own or their customers' expenditure on investment.

This view seems to have had as yet no supporter in the Economic Section or anywhere else in the Treasury. The summer forecast,[63] finalised on 6 July did, it is true, show some fall in total fixed investment during 1962, and, as compared with February, a much bigger fall in stock-building, and very little growth of gross domestic product. But for 1963 it remained optimistic, expecting a rise in fixed investment, a large recovery in stocks and work in progress, and a further big rise in exports. In a note for the Budget Committee and the Chancellor dated 26 June[64] Mr Cairncross argued that the expected growth in 1962 had been delayed by various special factors, but was now getting under way. He pointed to a steady rise in new car registrations and in bank advances to private borrowers, which would be accelerated by the recent relaxation of hire purchase controls; he thought this would raise demand by £60/80 million, equal to using about one-third of the regulator. He expected a further rise in exports, and thought that the fall in manufacturing investment would be more than offset by more public investment.

The Chancellor seems to have accepted this diagnosis without comment. After explaining it to the Cabinet on 27 June, he said flatly that he thought it unnecessary to contemplate any measures to stimulate expansion beyond those already taken; if anything had to be done later, it should be by monetary means and not by using the regulator in reverse or by increasing government expenditure. The Cabinet minutes show that the Prime Minister and some other members were restive. There were in particular murmurs about unemployment in Scotland and the north-east, and about a lack of confidence in industry, which had been increased by a fall in share prices. The Cabinet took note, and agreed to resume discussion later. The Chancellor was clearly shaken. He told Sir Frank Lee that he was under pressure to reflate, on the ground that the economy was stagnant and likely to get worse. He still did not want to increase consumption, but mentioned accelerated depreciation allowances (a favourite idea of the Prime Minister) to help investment. Sir Frank Lee told him that he did not think reflationary action was necessary. If ministers did decide to act, he would prefer to stimulate investment rather than consumption, but he did not think that accelerated depreciation allowances would do this, at least in the short term. This line was unanimously approved at a small Treasury meeting on the following day.[65] The minutes of the next Cabinet, on 5 July, only record a correction by the Chancellor of the previous minutes: while it was true that he had not then thought that measures to stimulate expansion were necessary, he did not exclude the possibility that they might became so. The responsibility soon ceased to be his: on 13 July Mr Maudling became Chancellor in his stead.

III
The 'Cure by Growth', July 1962 to December 1963

The new Chancellor, Mr Maudling, was aged 47. He was thus a much younger man than his two predecessors had been when they took office: Amory had been 60, Mr Selwyn Lloyd 58. He was sympathetic to the ideas about the necessity for more rapid economic growth, which had become widespread in industry and the trade unions, and which were voiced in the NEDC. He had a strong intellectual interest in the business of managing the economy, and he was well aware of its complexities. Later on he took calculated risks, particularly with the balance of payments, but he did not do this without careful and often lengthy consideration of the odds, and as part of a strategy which he always envisaged for two or more years ahead. It was widely expected that his appointment would mean a change of economic policy; but this was publicly denied, and in fact he took no immediate action. The Treasury submission of 17 July[66] advised delay. He spent most of August and early September in the office, questioning both officials and industrialists, and pressing forward consideration of both old and new devices for stimulating the economy when the need became certain.

During July, views changed inside the Treasury. As early as 6 July Mr Cairncross recorded a talk with Mr Maurice Allen and Mr O'Brien of the Bank of England, in which they were sceptical of his view that production would expand considerably in the next few months. They feared that the fall in manufacturing investment would be larger than the Treasury forecast allowed for, and that it would have big secondary effects. The Economic Section (Mr Godley) then worked out the implications of taking a rather more gloomy view of private investment (including housing and distribution as well as industry). This would reduce the rate of growth of the gross domestic product in the financial year from 4.5 to 3.5 per cent and by rather more during 1963, with unemployment rising rather than falling as forecast. But he did not believe that this would happen, and thought that all that was needed now was a firm statement by the Chancellor that the aim remained, as stated at budget time, a rise of 4 per cent in 1962/63 and that any measures necessary to get it would be taken.

Sir Frank Lee's submission of 17 July did explain that there were big uncertainties about the extent and effects of a fall in manufacturing investment, and about the impact of an American recession upon exports. But he endorsed the Budget Committee's recommendation that 'there is no case for taking any immediate steps to increase demand', and that decisions should therefore be deferred until the end of September, when the prospects would be clearer. On 31 July, however, Mr Cairncross told the Budget Committee that the latest information especially about rising unemployment and a change of mood in industry 'now greatly weakens the presumption against taking action in the near future to stimulate domestic demand'; and Sir Frank Lee summed up that 'today the risks of inaction look more formidable than those of action'.[70] But the regulator was now out of action for the recess, and bank rate could not be reduced at once for external reasons, so no action was recommended.

The Chancellor did not not get much light from his talk with industrialists on 9 August. All agreed that the confidence of industry needed to be restored, but were divided about how this should be done; and, as the note-takers said afterwards, 'the noise of grinding axes filled the room'. Nevertheless, on 23 August the Chancellor told Sir Frank Lee that, although he did not think immediate action necessary, it might be right to announce a 'package' in his Mansion House speech on 2 October, after his return from the meeting of the International Monetary Fund in New York. Preparations for this 'package' went forward on the lines of a list suggested by the Chancellor in a minute of 5 September. On the monetary side, he suggested a reduction of bank rate, and a release of 1 of the special deposits coupled with a directive to the clearing banks to give priority to advances to exporters and to firms in development districts, but not to expand too fast. For public investment an extra £60 million should be authorised for school building and a big fillip given to the power stations programme. On the fiscal side, there might be a release, of post-war credits by lowering the age limit by three years; and something should be done, but later, about depreciation allowances to encourage industrial investment. All this was cautious enough, still tentative, and, apart from the expansion of public investment, easily reversible.

Officials were still uncertain about the underlying trend. At the end of August, Mr Cairncross reported that the figures of industrial production for June had shown a further rise, and that de-stocking seemed to have stopped. The picture was more reassuring than at the end of July. I should think it right to give the economy a jolt now only, or primarily, as a gesture.' In late September he still advised delay before any decision to take drastic action, to see whether the levelling out of the rise in unemployment in August and September was maintained.

Most of the Chancellor's list of reflationary measures were duly announced around 3 October, though the Bank, after a tussle, kept bank rate unchanged at 4.5 per cent, mainly to help its relations with other central banks. But pressure for more was strengthened by the October unemployment figures. These showed a rise of 38,000 to 2.2 per cent and were 131,000 above the level a year earlier. Mr Cairncross minuted the Chancellor that, in view of these figures, 'we ought to reconsider the case for drastic action to expand demand, using the regulator to the fullest extent'.[71] The Budget Committee, now headed by Mr William Armstrong, who had just succeeded Sir Frank Lee as Permanent Secretary, took a more restrained view. They pointed out that, on the latest figures, production, consumption, and bank advances were still rising; and they attributed the rise in unemployment to a 'continuing shake-out of labour, which is good in the long run'. They advised against using the regulator or making any general reduction of purchase tax. It had been conveniently remembered that individual rates of purchase tax could be altered by Treasury Order, and the Committee recommended that the rate for cars should be reduced from to 45 to 25 per cent, thus bringing it into line with the rate for other consumable durables and helping an industry which was in special difficulties, though not mainly concentrated in areas of high unemployment. The Chancellor agreed to this, but also decided, in the face of strong protest from the Inland Revenue and doubts from the Treasury, to operate on depreciation allowances in order to stimulate industrial investment, whose decline was recognised as the main cause for anxiety. In the debate on the economic situation on 5 November, after announcing the reduction of purchase tax on cars, he said that in the 1963 Finance Bill investment allowances on machinery would be increased from 20 to 30 per cent, and on industrial buildings from 10 to 15 per cent, and the annual depreciation rates on new heavy plant improved; the new rates would apply to all relevant expenditure made after the date of this announcement. These measures were followed before the end of the year by the release of the last £80 million of special deposits on 29 November; by permission on 17 December for local authorities in Merseyside, Scotland and the north-east coast to start 'winter employment' capital works; and, as a New Year offering, by the reduction to 25 per cent of purchase tax on radio and television sets, records, and cosmetics.

Thus ended the first two stages in measures which had developed fast from a mere relaxation of restraints to a full-blooded injection of positive stimuli by the Government. The cost of the immediate fiscal concessions was expected to be about £130 million in a year – £42 million for repayment of post-war credits, £55-62 million for the reduction of purchase tax on cars, £25-30 million for other purchase tax reductions. The cost of the additional investment allowances would only be felt in 1964 and later, though it was hoped that they would give an early stimulus to orders for investment goods. The increases in public investment specially authorised in October amounted to £70 million, with a further £10 million for 'winter capital works' authorised in December, but the change in policy certainly affected other public investment programmes as well. The money supply was also directly increased by the release of £80 million of special deposits, and the mobilisation of this was eased by the withdrawal of the restrictions on bank lending. But as in 1958 there seems to have been little attempt to calculate in advance either the likely total effect on expenditure, or even when particular measures would make their impact felt; nor, apart from the Chancellor's determination to raise investment allowances, was there any direct attempt to check the decline in private investment. The stress was rather on raising final demand, expanding public investment to fill the gap left by the fall in private investment, and on restoring confidence in the need for more capacity in the future. Some attempt was, indeed, made at first to confine new authorisations to work in areas of high employment; but this restraint did not last long. It is interesting to see that the Chief Secretary (Mr Boyd Carpenter) distrusted the wide sweep of the measures. In a minute to the Chancellor of 10 December[70] he observed that 'the appetite of colleagues for expenditure to deal with unemployment has very real dangers, especially since, already, the 1963/64 Estimates will be 10 per cent above those for 1962/63'. He thought that the quickest and safest instrument was the reduction of taxation – and further decisions to increase expenditure could remove the possibility of this from the budget. 'Moreover, no public expenditure authorised now can affect employment before April, while most of it will affect 1964/65, in what may well be the opposite direction to what is then wanted. Therefore, until April, rely on what has been done; and, in April, do what then seems right in the budget.' There was much practical sense, if no refined theory, in this advice.

The NIF report of 3 December[71] gave grounds for some further reflation. It said that since early in 1962 both demand and production had risen quite substantially, but that unemployment had diverged; and its rise had been larger, and had continued longer, than had been expected. The economy was therefore now running below capacity. But, taking into account the stimulus already given, the authors forecast that both domestic demand and production would rise by nearly 3 per cent between the third quarters of 1962 and 1963. They also thought that total fixed investment would be 1 per cent higher by the third quarter of 1963, and might then begin to rise faster; and that stock building might also rise. They did not, however, expect much growth of exports, and the balance of payments forecast suggested an improvement of only £100 million after a small surplus in 1962. It thus seemed that in 1963 the economy would grow at, or nearly at, the long-term trend rate, but would start from a level which contained some slack and would therefore permit, for a time, a faster growth.

In commenting on this to the Budget Committee,[72] Mr Cairncross pointed to two main uncertainties: was the margin of spare resources really as large, and growing as fast, as the October and November unemployment figures suggested? And how would confidence abroad react to our reflation, when the balance of payments prospect was poor and a successful end to our bid to join the Common Market very doubtful? On the whole, he thought that the rise in unemployment was due to release of 'hoarded' labour, rather than to any general recession; but he nonetheless suggested further expansionary action to take it up. To expand demand by 2 per cent more would require a fiscal release of purchasing power of about £300 million; by 3 per cent, £500 million. Either would mean taking risks with the balance of payments. Nevertheless, he advocated a £300 million release, beginning with the use of the regulator before Christmas. This was much too strong meat for the Budget Committee. They insisted on toning down his appraisal, recommended against the use of the regulator (which the Chancellor was now known to dislike), and insisted on the omission of any precise figure for a budget release. In this form it was sent to the Chancellor on 10 December.[73] It may have encouraged but probably did not determine, his decision to make the further reductions of purchase tax which were announced on 31 December.

The New Year began with a series of studies inside the Treasury of how much further reflation ought to go, and of how its pace could later be moderated as the present slack in the economy was taken up: it was clearly essential to avoid a repetition of the events of 1960 and 1961. As has been said, the Economic Section had, early in 1962, analysed the reflation of 1958/59. This paper was now turned into a comparative study of this experience with what had so far been done, and what might still be needed, in 1962 and

1963;[74] and it was then circulated by the Chancellor to the Economic Policy Committee. After some divisions of opinion in the Treasury, it was concluded that the effects of the measures taken so far were likely to be a good deal less than those of 1958 and 1959, and also that an export boom like that of 1959 was very improbable. So far, we were not in danger of having done too much. But one of the lessons of 1958/60 was that measures large enough to have a dramatic effect on demand and production must generate multiplier increases which were hard to quantify and hard to control. The paper pointed out, very wisely, that the effect of a given dose of any measure was not automatic, and had to be guessed at in the light of the general circumstances. Thus the relaxation of severe hire-purchase restrictions in 1958 had great effect because there was much pent-up desire for consumer durables; but relaxations from a lesser severity in 1962 seemed to have had only small effect. Similarly, though 'personal and professional' bank advances had risen by £320 million from 1958 to 1960, so fast a rise was not likely to be repeated now because lending was already high. (In the event, they grew from 1962 to 1964 from £707 million to £991 million – rather less absolutely, and very much less proportionately to the starting level.)

The February 1963 NIF report[75] differed in one major particular from that of November, in that it recorded lower levels in the second half of 1962, with an actual fall of production in the last quarter. In 1963 the economy would therefore start with more spare capacity, both of machinery and labour. The authors had, however, no doubt that the downward trend had been, or very shortly would be, reversed; and they forecast for 1963, without further stimuli, much the same rate of growth as before, with gross domestic product rising between the second halves of 1962 and 1963 by 3.25 per cent, and rather more slowly between the last quarters. There would be a further moderate rise in unemployment in the first half of the year, which would then flatten out. They expected a sharper rise in consumer spending early in the year, and a bigger growth of fixed investment later; but they apparently thought that the former would die away unless given some further deliberate stimulus. The report rather strengthened the case for an expansionary budget. So did the simultaneous set-back to production and morale which came from the abnormal winter weather, and which pushed the crude unemployment up to 933,000 (UK) in February.

Mr Cairncross took a strongly expansionist line when he expounded to the Budget Committee on 15 February[76] the results of the Economic Section's study and the NIF report. There were three key questions: how fast should we like production to rise? How fast would it rise without further acts of policy? How much needed to be done to add a defined amount to production over a given period? On the first question, he estimated the normal growth in capacity at 3 per cent to 3.5 per cent, perhaps more, and the present 'slack' at about the same amount, giving a total margin a year ahead of around 7 per cent. But this, on the experience of 1958/59, could not safely be taken up in one year, since expansion must fall to the normal capacity growth rate as resources became strained. He thought that a 10 per cent growth in production by the first quarter of 1965 might be attainable, with a target of 4 per cent for 1963. Of this he thought (implicitly writing down the NIF conclusions), only a half would be attained without further stimuli. There was, however, something of a dilemma. If too much slack were taken up in 1963, the much-needed expansion of exports and up-turn of industrial investment in 1964 could not be met; but if these did not materialise, a very large stimulus to home demand would be needed in 1964. To the third question he gave no direct answer; but in December he had said that to raise demand by 2 per cent (about £570 million at current prices) would require a budgetary release of £300 million, by 3 per cent of £500 million. He now recommended budget cuts of £250 million, but with the rider that preparations should be made, and the intention stated, to do more later if this became necessary.

Some members of the Committee were uneasy about this recommendation. It seemed too much for the balance of payments and yet too little to reduce unemployment quickly to a level which ministers would regard as tolerable. Sir William Armstrong suggested that we were getting into a position where a weak balance of payments was associated with high unemployment and not only with excess demand, as heretofore; but no one then thought it right to discuss devaluation as the remedy. Moreover, there were budgetary difficulties. The Supply Estimates for 1963/64 were up by £527 million (9.4 per cent) and the tax remissions suggested would mean budgeting for a deficit of £100 million above the line. No one now raised doctrinal objections to this, but the Treasury were afraid of its effect on confidence abroad. A further point, which neither Mr Cairncross nor the Committee took, was that the recently announced increases in National Insurance benefits and contributions (outside the budget), were quite considerably inflationary. Over a full year about £180 million more than before would be transferred from contributors to beneficiaries, whose propensity to spend was certainly higher than that of the contributors; and there would be also a once-for-all effect, worth about £20 million, because the increase in benefits applied from 7 March and that in contributions only on 3 June.

In spite of these doubts, Sir William Armstrong broadly endorsed Mr Cairncross's reasoning in his submission to the Chancellor,[77] and recommended tax reductions of between £200 million and £300 million, in addition to the cost of the purchase tax reductions which had been made by Order in November and December. He described this as a middle course between budgeting for balance above the line, which would limit tax remissions to £150 million, and giving concessions of £400 million, which had been publicly advocated by the National Institution of Economic and Social Research. Even so, the expected overall deficit of £150 million in the balance of payments would be worsened. 'Much would depend on whether the budget could be presented as part of a concerted attack on the long-term problems of the economy.' The Chancellor was worried by the balance of payments aspect of this, but after further discussion took the view that a deficit caused in part by re-stocking materials in advance of a planned rise in production, and in part by abnormal items of investment abroad, could be treated as temporary and met if necessary by drawings from the International Monetary Fund. He recognised that this was a calculated gamble, which could only succeed if the rise in imports were moderate and if exports grew substantially later in 1963 and in 1964. He did, therefore, ask for a study of possible emergency measures if things went wrong, and held a meeting on 13 March of Treasury ministers and officials, but without the Bank of England, to consider them. The Chancellor himself said that he would prefer import surcharges to import controls, and there was some discussion about whether powers to impose these should be taken now in the Finance Act, or only if and when they were needed for use. Export incentives had the advantage of being positive instead of merely restrictive but no scheme which would be both administratively practicable and quick acting had yet been found. He said he was attracted by multiple currency devices such as those which France had used; but it was objected that these would inevitably be regarded as a preliminary to devaluation. 'Discussion passed quickly over floating rates and devaluation.'

The Chancellor broadly accepted Sir William Armstrong's advice about the total size of the budget's tax concession for 1963/64, though he chose a figure nearer the upper than the lower end of the £200-£300 million bracket. On 3 April he announced reductions estimated to cost £269 million in all during 1963/63. The main items were the abolition of Schedule A income tax on the assessed value of owner-occupied houses, which had been promised by his predecessor a year before (£35 million); other changes in income tax (£198 million), mainly from the raising of allowances and exemption limits, benefiting largely the lower income groups; and reductions in Estate Duty and Stamp Duties (£27.75 million), the latter being expected to help the raising of new capital and the buying and selling of houses. Reductions in customs and excise duties were very small, beyond the cuts in purchase tax which had already been made by Treasury Order before the New Year. In a full year the total cost was expected to be much greater – £638 million, partly because of the delayed effect on surtax yield of the higher allowances, but mainly because the cost of increased investment and initial allowances which had been announced in November, and the new grant of 'free depreciation' of investment by firms in development districts, would only begin to show appreciably in 1964/65 and thereafter. The Inland Revenue put the annual future cost at £200 million and £40 million respectively. The tax cuts produced an estimated deficit of £90 million above the line for 1963/64. The overall deficit, at £687 million, looked huge, but the Chancellor expected that much of this could be met from National Savings and the surpluses of public funds, without much recourse to borrowing in the market. The Finance Bill also provided for renewal of the customs and excise 'regulator'. The use of this was made slightly easier by reductions (but not increases) subject to affirmative resolution within 21 sitting days, instead of calendar days.

The novelty in the budget was the geographically limited grant of 'free depreciation' of the costs of new plant and machinery. This, like the raising of the investment allowances, had been strongly opposed by the Inland Revenue, who were supported on the whole by the Treasury. The Chancellor first mooted the idea, as a means of giving a general stimulus to industrial investment, at a meeting in September; and on 16 October he received a note from the Prime Minister inquiring about its possibilities.[78] The Inland Revenue objected that the cost would be prohibitive. Industry was then investing about

£1,500 million a year, so that, as long as firms had enough profits against which to charge the depreciation, annual tax receipts of around £700 million to £800 million would be at risk if they were given freedom to treat the whole of their new investment as a cost in one year. They further argued (as they did also on investment allowances) that, though this concession would certainly give industry larger current net profits, it would not necessarily persuade them to alter investment plans, which, the Inland Revenue thought, depended much more on firms' assessments of future profitability than on their immediate cash flow. In December the Ministerial Committee on Population and Employment asked the Chancellor to look at the possibility of giving free depreciation as a selective concession deliberately designed to divert more new investment to areas of high unemployment.[79] The introduction of geographic disorientation in taxation would be a startling innovation. But it would not cost as much as a general concession, and as a directional stimulus it might be very effective. Early in January the Budget Committee recommended against the idea,[80] their main points being that capital assistance to firms in making investment, such as was already given by the Board of Trade in the development districts, was a better stimulus than giving relief to chargeable profits which might not be made; that the concession would have to be given to all new investment in the relevant areas, whereas the Board of Trade, acting selectively could achieve better results at smaller cost; that there was a strong body of opinion against such discriminatory use of taxation, which had been rejected even for Scotland by the Toothill Committee; and, finally, that it would be very difficult to decide, and still more difficult to maintain, the boundaries of the benefiting areas, especially before decisions were taken about the proposed 'growth zones' in central Scotland and on the north-east coast. On 1 January, however, the Chancellor minuted that 'he found these reasons strong but not conclusive', and asked for further study. On 24 February he decided to adopt the proposal, and on 27 March he accepted a suggestion from the President of the Board of Trade that it should apply within any development districts scheduled then or in future under the Local Employment Act. The concession applied to expenditure on new plant and machinery (but not to buildings) made in these areas after budget day. It lasted until it was superseded by investment grants in January 1966. The Inland Revenue later estimated that its total cost for that period was £77 million, building up to a peak of £45 million in 1965/66. It is not possible to disentangle its effects from those of the increased grants for industrial buildings and the new 10 per cent grant for plant and machinery, which were offered selectively under the Local Employment Act at the same time. But the information later collected by the Board of Trade does suggest that, coming just before a general up-turn of industrial investment, 'free depreciation' did have a considerable effect in deflecting some of this to the development districts. In so far as, in the long run, it evened up the distribution of resources and employment, it would help the general control of demand. But it was clearly not an instrument which could be easily used in reverse if general pressures again became excessive.

The Chancellor did his best to present the budget as part of a wider plan for growth, modernisation of the economy and a serious attempt to build up centres of growth in the backward parts of the country; and to counter the suspicion that the Government was once again merely seeking to spend its way out of trouble.

The theme is expansion; expansion without inflation; expansion that can be sustained ... The purpose is to do the Government's part in achieving the rate of growth broadly described as the 4 per cent target, which we have already accepted in the NEDC.*[81]

No more measures of deliberative reflation were announced, or needed, after the budget of 1963, though additions to public investment programmes and to current public expenditure went on apace, despite the endeavours of the Treasury to check them. At the end of May a 'swap' currency credit of $500 million was agreed with the US Federal Reserve, to replace a similar arrangement which had covered only a tenth of this amount; and in August a stand-by credit of £357 million, was negotiated with the International Monetary Fund, in addition to the drawing of about £100 million which had been made in March. These measures strengthened the power of the Bank to deal with strains on the exchanges from the rise in imports which had already begun, or from confidence movements. Bank rate remained at 4 per cent, to which it had been reduced on 3 January.

The NIF report of 10 July[82] forecast the growth of gross domestic product at 5.2 per cent between the last quarters of 1962 and 1963, and at 5.5/6 per cent between the second quarters of 1963 and 1964 with a further rise during the rest of 1964. These were high rates of expansion, but the forecast does not seem to have caused any alarm. At a meeting with the Chancellor on 15 July the TUC pressed for further measures of expansion, but the Chancellor pointed out to them that the budget income tax changes had still to be felt – because of the working of PAYE. £40 million would enlarge the pay packets in that very week. Their complaint that unemployment was still serious north of the Humber could not, however, be disputed. In the Economic Section's monthly survey Mr Hopkin gave, for the first time in this context, a table which showed clearly the rise, both absolute and relative, in the unemployment percentages in Scotland and in the northern region as compared with the south and Midlands. In July 1959 the percentages had been 1.2 in the south and Midlands, 2.9 in the northern region, and 4.0 in Scotland; in July 1963 they were 1.3, 4.0 and 4.3. Wales, however, had shown a clear improvement, with a fall from 3.3 per cent to 2.8 per cent; and Northern Ireland had remained constant at the high level of 7.2 per cent. He warned that 'free depreciation' and the 'growth zone' plans would of necessity take time to show results. In September Sir William Armstrong, commenting to the Chancellor on a paper by Mr Cairncross, said that the general impression was that expansion was a little faster than was expected at budget-time, but that there was still plenty of slack. The Bank of England took a less optimistic view than the Treasury and the Board of Trade. But the Budget Committee were unanimous that no regulatory action, up or down, was needed.

*   See an interesting note, 'Historical Memorandum on Reflation and Modernisation, 1962–63', prepared by Mr Wiggins in November 1964. This analyses the interaction of the 'Modernisation of Britain' ideas, launched by the Prime Minister in October 1962, with the measures of reflation. (2EAS 1/06 and PIO files.)

Within a month, however, warning notes began. On 17 October Mr Cairncross sent a minute[83] to the Chancellor expressing alarm at the present rate of expansion; and this was elaborated, but much toned down, in a note which went from the Chancellor to the new Prime Minister, Sir Alec Douglas Home, on 25 October. This note said that, although the present position was highly satisfactory, the level of demand was rising rapidly, and it was only a matter of time before the remaining slack was taken up. The White Paper on Public Investment, about to be published, would show an increase of 20 per cent in 1964/65 over 1963/64. The informed public would soon begin to ask when restraining action was contemplated, and in what form. No sensational improvement in the regional problems could be expected for a year or two; and the size of current wage increases, about 5.5 per cent, was accelerating. The balance of payments outlook was for 1964 relatively promising, but 'as the pressure of demand increases we are bound to move into a more anxious period.'

On 15 November, in a paper for the Budget Committee covering the latest forecast,[84] Mr Cairncross was more forthright. It was now 'almost inconceivable' that the expansion forecast of 8.5 per cent from the second half of 1963 to the end of 1964, with a fairly steady rate of 5.5 per cent, could be matched by resources for as long as 18 months; and the momentum was increasing. Already 'some weakening' of the balance of payments was expected in 1964 with perhaps loss of confidence and an outflow of funds as well. He concluded that the brakes should be put on before 1964. This process might start with a stiffer attitude to public investment, some check to private non-industrial building, perhaps the imposition of fees for building starts in 1964, a refurbishing of the regulator, followed by some increase in profits tax and indirect taxation in the budget. These would be forward-looking measures, mostly aimed at giving an early check to investment plans which would otherwise increase expenditure late in 1964 and in 1965. The Budget Committee were inclined to agree with him, but felt that it could not yet put such a forecast to ministers on the confident assumption that it was correct, and that it was no use to advise restraining measures until ministers had fully accepted the diagnosis. Despite this hesitation, however, the Chancellor put a warning paper on the economy and the worsening balance of payments to the Economic Policy Committee before Christmas. That Committee does not seem to have bean much impressed. But the Chancellor personally drafted a paper for Cabinet on December which began by saying flatly:

We are facing the problem of how to control a boom ... We have been here before (in 1960 and 1961). But this time our resources to sustain the £ are greater; we have a better control over the internal money situation; and we are tackling the problem of incomes earlier and with much greater public understanding.

He closed, however, on rather a weak note:

We shall have several months in hand in which to develop effective policies for controlling the boom, but the measures needed to do this will not be popular.

He did not at that meeting even ask for restraint of public investment. The Wages Committee was asked to strengthen resistance to breaches of incomes policy; and the

Secretary of State for Industry (Mr Heath) to consider reduction or suspension of tariffs, and policy on resale price maintenance and monopolies, as possible contributors to keep prices stable.

Thus the year 1963 ended with return to restriction of demand clearly in sight but with doubts both among officials and ministers as to how soon, and by what means, it should begin. The Government was pledged to policies of growth, moderation, and the redevelopment of the north-east coast and central Scotland; and a general election was inevitable within ten months. To check the momentum now would clearly be difficult and bitter. The course of the reflation was a humbling experience, for the Treasury as well as for ministers. As Hopkin commented[85] on 18 December, in spite of the conclusions drawn from 1958 and 1959, we now had a growth of output at very nearly the same excessive rate; we had underestimated the growth of exports in 1963 as in 1959, though not by quite as much; and, though we had recognised that a series of measures, by interacting and multiplying, could exceed the total of each taken separately, the size and speed of the response to them certainly been more than we expected. And, though he did not know it then, the rise in imports, which had been expected to be short-lived, was much larger and went on much longer than had been forecast.

IV

Controlling the Boom, January to October 1964

Throughout January Mr Cairncross's minutes to the Chancellor continued to stress the inevitability of restrictive measures by, or before, the autumn, in order to lower the rate of domestic expansion as the margin of slack disappeared. He did not, however, at this stage, lay much stress on the external problem. There would be a substantial loss of reserves, beginning probably about the middle of the year; but 'given rising exports and rising costs on the Continent, we ought to be able to deal with any sterling crisis in 1964 with the help of our friends'[86] (i.e. the other central banks and the IMF), though there might be serious doubts before the autumn about 1965. He did not again press for immediate action, beyond the throttling down of public expenditure, which the Treasury was trying to secure by more than usually vigorous screening of the Estimates. Papers for the Economic Assessment Group, which had recently been formed under Sir William Armstrong's chairmanship, brought out starkly that, given present public expenditure policies and commitments, over the period 1964 to 1967 an extra £100 million of taxation a year would be needed on average even to balance the budget. Mr Goldman also put to the Group on 14 January proposals for an early increase of 1 per cent of bank rate, both to get back in line with the United States Federal Reserve rate, and to discourage stock building and the demand for houses at home.[87] Mr Cairncross and others, however, feared the effect of this upon industrial investment. Sir William Armstrong summed up against the proposal, but remarked that if it were not adopted 'we should have to reconcile ourselves to a greater leakage of short-term funds abroad', and that the problem of how to take 'mild and early action' to restrain consumer demand would remain. The Chancellor decided 'to do nothing for the time being'; but under pressure from the Bank the rate was in fact raised from 4 per cent to 5 per cent on 27 February. As in 1960, this was the first overtly restrictive move.

On 31 January the Budget Committee discussed a preliminary assessment by Mr Cairncross, made in advance of the final conclusions of the NIF and Balance of Payments Working Parties.[88] He emphasised the unexpectedly rapid fall in unemployment, apparently unaccompanied by a fully corresponding increase in production. By April unemployment would probably be down to 1.7 per cent (350,000 GB). This would begin to reproduce the mid-1961 labour shortage and would also leave room for an effective incomes policy. He thought now that there ought to be an increase of taxation of £50–100 million, to slow the rate of increase of demand to 4 per cent. If nothing were done in the budget, either the use of the regulator during the summer, or an autumn budget, would become inevitable. The Committee did not disagree with this diagnosis. Most members, however, took the view that the 'politically feasible' choice lay between a neutral budget and an increase of taxation of £50 million at the outside. The NIF appraisal and forecast,[89] which were considered on 17 February, broadly confirmed those of December; but the latest balance of payments forecast was for an overall deficit of £400 million in 1964, with no clear sign of improvement in 1965. The Budget Committee were depressed. Sir Alexander Johnston (Inland Revenue) thought that nothing less than a £200 million increase would have much effect. The Committee agreed that at least £100 million was necessary, but doubted if it were practicable, especially if the date of the election necessitated a short and uncontroversial Finance Bill.[90] Sir William Armstrong's submission to the Chancellor, which advised this increase, mentioned that experience suggested that a fall in unemployment to below 1.7 per cent would be accompanied by a rapid further rise in wage costs, which would undermine our competitive position and make the balance of payments once again the check on sustained growth in the economy.

The Chancellor, in discussions on 2 and 8 March, readily accepted this judgement of the economic requirements, and also said firmly that the prospect of an early election must not prevent necessary increase in taxation though he ruled out any change in personal taxation; and on 8 March he said that an October election could be assumed, and agreed to an increase of around £100 million in indirect taxation, keeping the regulator in reserve and making it more flexible. In preparation for this he put on 24 March a note to the Economic Policy Committee,[91] covering an official summary of the latest forecasts for 1964 and a warning that for both 1964 and 1965, a large balance of payments deficit seemed inevitable.

Our conclusion is that there is an underlying weakness in the economy which makes it extremely difficult to combine a reasonably full use of productive potential with a viable balance of payments.

The budget of 14 April increased taxation net by an estimated £103 million in 1964/65 and £116 million in a full year, almost entirely from drink, tobacco and rental charges to independent television contractors. It provided for an above the line surplus of £67 million and an overall deficit of £791 million; but about £160 million of the latter represented a transfer of local authority borrowing from the market to the Public Works Loans Board. The Finance Bill also renewed the powers to use the regulator, but made them more flexible by allowing the exclusion from its use on any occasion of any of the major blocks – tobacco, alcohol, oil, purchase tax – though not allowing surcharges or rebates on them at different rates. The outturn for 1963/4 had been favourable: expenditure above the line had, for once, fallen short of the estimate, and there had been a surplus of £73 million instead of the expected deficit. The borrowing requirement had also been lower by about £200 million. Thus the budgetary stimulus to the economy given in 1963, though it had proved to be excessive, had actually turned out to be considerably less than was planned.

The budget was politically more courageous than officials had thought possible when they tendered their advice in January and February. The Chancellor described its main purpose – and the main reason for the increased taxation – as being 'to achieve a smooth transition from the recent exceptionally rapid rate of growth to the long-term growth rate of 4 per cent'.[92] This reiterated the long-term objective which the Government had accepted a year earlier, though most official advice, both before and since, was that it was unrealistically high and could not be sustained once the margin of slack had been absorbed, probably before the end of 1964. The Chancellor also laid some stress on the fact that, because of another big jump of £410 million (6.7 per cent) in the Estimates, increased taxation was necessary if he were to avoid budgeting for a deficit above the line for two years in succession.

The Government still had six months of life, and it was seven months before its successor introduced a second budget and had to face another crisis for sterling. Through the early summer and up to the recess, official advice was on the whole reassuring. In late May, the latest figures suggested that production had risen by 2.5 per cent in the first quarter of 1964 over the last quarter of 1963, that fixed investment was still rising and stock-building was still high. But imports were said to be 'on a slightly slower upward trend' – as well they might be, since they had risen from £360 million in the month of January 1963 to £455 million in April 1964. Exports had risen by about 5 per cent in the last three months, though 'the underlying trend is probably less'. The demand for labour was still growing, but the numbers of adults unemployed still exceeded vacancies by 175,000, as compared with 560,000 in March 1963; there was still a little slack in the labour market. Mr Cairncross's conclusion, given to the Chancellor on 1 and 4 June in preparation for a talk with the Prime Minister and as a brief for a meeting with economic journalists, was quite definite: 'We do not think that pressure generated over the summer will be plainly excessive, or that some easing of pressure thereafter can be ruled out; but we do expect an increasingly tight labour market'.[93] The brief for the OECD Working Party Number 3 in early June had much the same story.

By July some easement seemed actually in sight. The NIF report,[94] dated 1 July, began by saying: 'it seems fairly clear that the pace of expansion has been moderating somewhat in the first half of 1964 ... The general outlook is for a slacking to a rate in 1965 roughly in line with the assumed growth of potential, just over 3 per cent'. The main immediate sign of the slackening was that industrial production was thought to have been only 1 per cent higher during February to April than in the preceding three months, after rising almost without a wobble for 12 months by over 12 per cent. Job vacancies and unemployment also seemed to have changed less in the second quarter than in the first. This slackening in production was attributed to some sluggishness in the demand from consumers, perhaps associated with rising prices, including those resulting from the budget; and to less stock-building. The report did not note, as it might have done, that, on its own figures, the rise in imports in the first half of 1964 was equal to two-thirds of the total estimated increase in final expenditure, though it forecast a much smaller rise in future. But business confidence was said to be still high, and exports and fixed investment were rising strongly. For the future, the authors expected unemployment to fall by a further 50,000 to about 300,000 – barely 1.4 per cent – by the middle of 1965. The report itself gave no warnings and drew no morals for policy; but the implication was that things were now beginning to work according to plan. On 9 July a paper from the Bank of England,[95] reporting the views of the clearing banks, also indicated that expansion was going on steadily but not excessively, except perhaps in building and the car industry; and that business confidence was high. At the end of month there was even some alarm lest the slackening of expansion might become excessive, since the index of production had remained almost flat for the first five months of the year, and exports had increased little during the second quarter. Mr Cairncross devoted most of his appraisal to the Chancellor on 23 July to showing that such alarm was unfounded. Exports could still rise later, and the growth of imports 'no more than matches production' (surely, on the evidence then available, an astonishing statement). The balance of payments deficit for the second half of the year would be over £300 million, but 'this was more or less as expected'.

The implication that all was well could not, however, be easily accepted in the Treasury, particularly in view of the worsening of balance of payments, both actual and prospective. In a paper dated 6 July[96] and discussed by the Budget Committee four days later, Mr Cairncross emphasised that, though the new NIF forecast was for a more moderate rate of growth of GDP – just under 4 per cent between the first halves of 1964 and 1965 and 3.25 per cent between the second halves – this still meant a continuing rise in the pressure of demand. If 4 per cent were really (as the Government had said) a sustainable rate of growth, and 1.5 per cent a workable minimum for unemployment this was acceptable. But if (as most officials thought) the figures were nearer 3.2 and 1.8 per cent, pressure was already too high, with seasonally corrected unemployment down to 1.7 per cent in June. And the slowing of growth had not prevented a large deterioration in the balance of payments. The overall deficit in the first quarter had been £150 million, and the latest forecast envisaged for the whole year a deficit of £260 million on current account and £600 million overall, with a further gap of £100 million and £290 million for 1965. The worst feature was 'an underlying weakness, which makes it unlikely that exports can overtake imports for at least two or three years, or the net capital outflow be kept below £200 million.' He concluded that the need for some action to right the balance of payments could hardly be disputed. When was a matter of political judgement. But, to avoid aggravation, 'some action to trim the growth of demand is called for as soon as possible.'

The Budget Committee agreed with this assessment, and Sir William Armstrong's submission to the Chancellor discussed three possible measures.[97] A regulator surcharge could be put on oil and purchase tax before the summer recess. This would be a significant restraint on the growth of demand. But it would give a shock to confidence, which might deter investment important for the future growth of the economy. Moreover, demand for consumer durables was not growing excessively, and an increase in the oil duty would be attacked as raising costs. Second, bank rate could be raised. This would strengthen the external position as well as restraining activity at home. But it would be unpopular abroad, particularly with the United States monetary authorities. It would be better held in reserve to deal with a possible run on sterling later. Finally, there could be a call on the banks to make 1 per cent special deposits. Since their liquidity ratio was already around 29 per cent (against the conventional minimum of 30 per cent), this would exercise distinct pressure on them to discourage marginal lending. It would have to be presented as a move to check demand as a whole, though there could be favourable treatment of borrowing for exports and for investment. This was recommended, for immediate action. The submission concluded, ominously,

we have accepted as overriding that any measures taken now should be consistent with the Government's present commitment to 4 per cent growth policy. But ... we believe that, within the next few months, there will have to be a major reappraisal of all our economic policies, followed by the preparation of public opinion for a different approach to economic growth, involving, in the interim, more severe measures of restraint.

The Chancellor, after some hesitation rejected this recommendation: he thought it politically unpresentable, against the background of the commitment to 4 per cent growth and the absence, as yet, of any sign of loss of confidence in sterling. Moreover, the recommendation unfortunately coincided with some alarm in the press and elsewhere, lest the apparent slackening of expansion was already excessive, since the index of industrial production had remained almost flat for the first five months of the year, and exports seemed to have risen little during the second quarter, though orders for them had done so. To administer a deliberate check to demand in these circumstances might provoke the very loss of confidence in sterling which it was intended to prevent.

The behaviour of the production index requires some comment. A sluggish index was in any case an ambiguous indicator. It could result either from a deficiency of demand and competitiveness; or from an overload which was creating bottlenecks and holding back production; or, again, the provisional figures could just be unrepresentative. In a minute of 13 July Mr Cairncross rather favoured the second explanation, drawing the parallel of what was believed to have happened in 1960. But in a fuller appraisal for the Chancellor on 23 July he relied more upon the third.[98] The overall balance of payments deficit for the second half of the year would be over £300 million, but 'this is more or less as now expected' in the latest BP Working Party forecast. Unemployment was still a good deal higher than the lowest rates reached in 1960/61, and it now looked as if there might be no further larger reduction in the autumn. On this, the last appraisal before the recess, the Chancellor commented: 'Very interesting and rather reassuring.'

In retrospect it is clear that the index of production was indeed very misleading over this period. The all-industries index (base 1958 and seasonally adjusted), published two months in arrears, remained flat at 126 from January to May as compared with a rise one point in each of the last three months of 1963. The August publication raised the whole flat level to 127, but only for September (published in November) was there a rise to 129. Successive revisions by 1968 and 1969 ended with a very different picture (see table below). If the later revisions are more to be trusted than the original figures, it seems that total industrial production was in fact rising during the first nine months of 1964 at an annual rate of 5 to 6 per cent, instead of remaining almost stationary. Had this been known at the time, the Budget Committee's recommendation for restraining action in July might well have prevailed.

	As revised by 1968 Base 1958	As published 1969, Base 1963, with 1963 weights
1963 4th quarter	124.0	104.1
1964 1st quarter	126.2	106.1
2nd quarter	127.9	108.0
3rd quarter	128.6	108.6
4th quarter	130.2	110.7

In August, some opinion outside Whitehall began to show alarm. In the middle of the month the NIESR published their appraisal for 1964 and 1965. As a comparison made by the Economic Section showed, their figures for 1964 differed little from those of the Treasury; but for 1965 they forecast an overall deficit of £450 million, instead of £300 million: much worse, not better, than in 1964. Their conclusion shifted the emphasis from present euphoria to future trouble:

Towards the end of 1964, Government will be faced with the old dilemma. It must either take measures which deal directly with balance of payments; or it must deflate, and face another period of stagnation.

This was much publicised. The *Financial Times* leader of 19 August was headed: 'Experts warn: trade crisis soon'. The *Guardian* on the same day argued for keeping expansion going, with the hope of reducing costs and improving industrial efficiency, and for facing a balance of payments crisis 'with equanimity': 'we should be prepared to borrow £350 million more abroad and to see the published reserves fall to £500 million, rather than drop farther behind other major industrial nations'. Few commentators openly mentioned devaluation. But the NIESR forecast was clear notice to importers and manufacturers to order all imports they might want while the going was good and bank rate still at 5 per cent; and arrivals for the rest of 1964 and into 1965 show that, even in the middle of the holiday season, they did the job.

In his first review after the holidays, on 18 September,[99] Mr Cairncross did, at last, put the emphasis on monetary factors and the balance of payments. Though production was flattening out at a record high level, money supply and bank advances were rising very fast, exports had checked, and the current balance of payments deficit was bigger than at any time since 1951. It had so far been supported by an in-flow of short-term capital, which 'is unlikely to continue'. On a rather longer view, if we had to eliminate an external deficit of £600 million from our own resources we should have to cut demand; and even if the deficit in 1965 were put at only £300 million (the figure used in July), 'it is difficult to see room for additional home demand'. There is no indication on the files of what the Chancellor or his colleagues thought of this. The election campaign was now upon them and, short of an overt crisis of the pound, remedial measures or a change of course could only wait for its result. But it is noteworthy that the general Treasury brief for the new Chancellor,[100] dated 23 October, did not suggest that the internal (as opposed to the external) situation out of hand. Industrial production was said to be on a plateau, and imports levelling out, though there was a 'pause' in the growth of exports. The mid-October figures showed that demand for labour was still rising. But there were 375,000 unemployed (1.5 per cent), still more than in October 1960. There was still some slack to be taken up, if only the strain on sterling could be first be held, then relieved. The need to cut back domestic demand to achieve this was not repeated: perhaps, in the circumstances, to state it was deemed a waste of ink.

In a note dated 30 November[101] Mr Cairncross asked, first, why the balance of payments had deteriorated so fast and so far? And, second, why production was rising so slowly and exports actually falling? He drew a close parallel with the position in 1960 and 1961: the stickiness of production after a period of over-rapid expansion, and the balance of payments difficulties, looked much the same. The rise in imports he attributed very largely to stock-building; as in 1960, this seemed to have jumped from about £100 million to £600 million in a year, while the visible trade balance deteriorated by about £400 million. But he also stressed pressure of demand as the cause, especially given the preference of British firms for meeting home rather than export orders:

it is arguable that, taking unemployment as a measure of the pressure of demand, the balance of payments will suffer much more when unemployment moves from 1.75 per cent to 1.5 per cent than from 2 per cent to 1.75 per cent.

He also attributed some of the imports to the sheer slowness of industry to adjust output to so rapid a rise in demand; and he admitted, but rather discounted, some 'loss of competitiveness' of home production, both against imports and in export markets. In discussing the current apparent stagnation of production, he mentioned shortages of labour and capacity in building and engineering, but thought the main cause was a rather slowly growing demand for consumer goods: 'consumer spending in the first nine months of 1964 has been not much more [presumably in real terms] than in the second half of 1963'. It is interesting that at no point in this appreciation did he mention the rapid rise of wages as a cause of the troubles of the economy, though the index of hourly wage rates rose by 7 points (5 per cent) between December 1963 and December 1964 with certainly very little increase in hourly output; and retail prices rose by about the same amount.

It is not easy even seven years later to judge the control of demand in the first nine months of 1964. It is obvious that reflation was overdone in the spring of 1963, so that expansion of demand went much too fast throughout that year. This brought an aftermath on the import side in 1964, and also probably accentuated the breakdown of the policy of wage restraint. But checks were imposed, if rather late, by the raising of bank rate in February and by the budget in April. At that time they may have been on about the right scale. Both the rise in imports, and the expansion of the economy, did ease somewhat during the summer, though the latter not as much as the provisional production figures misleadingly suggested. What seems to have been required at the end of July, or even as late as September, was a tightening of credit to damp down imports and stockbuilding and a determined attempt to regain some grip on the rise of wages and salaries. The impending election forbade such measures then. Perhaps some officials did not press their advice then only because they felt this to be so. In retrospect, it seems possible that, if action could have been taken at that time, the renewed flood of imports later in the year and the crisis of sterling could have been avoided and the growth of the economy brought to a sustainable rate of about 3.5 per cent in 1965, with more room for exports. The 'cure by growth' had always been a gamble with the balance of payments. The mistakes of early 1963 and the failure to maintain wage restraint later made the success of that gamble much more difficult. But it was probably the political vacuum of the summer of 1964 which clinched its failure.

Notes

1   EAS 31/04 H.
2   BD 59/03 A Hall to Makins, 8.5.59.
3   *Ibid.*, Hall to Makins, 16.7.58.
4   EAS 04 K. 19.12.58.
5   NIF (WP) (59) 2 Final, 12.2.58.
6   BC 59/03 A Hall to Padmore, 17.12.58.
7   NIF (WP) (59) 2 Final 23.2.59.
8   BC 59/03 B Hall to Makins, 24.2.59.
9   BC 59/04. Note of meeting with the Chancellor, 9.3.59.
10 BC 59/27.
11 BC (M) (59) 10.
12 Hansard, 7.4.59.
13 NIF (WP) (59) 5 Final.
14 BC (59) 33.
15 BC (60) 06. Makins to Chancellor, 29.7.59.
16 BC (60) 03, October 1959.
17 NIF (WP) (59) 10 Final.
18 BC (60) 02. Minutes, 14.12.59.
19 BC (60) 06. Makins to Chancellor, 15.12.59.
20 NIF (WP) (60) 1 Final, 9.2.60.
21 EA (60) 7, 28.1.60.
22 BC (60) 03, 12.2.60.
23 *Ibid.*, 12.2.60.
24 *Ibid.*, Financial Secretary to Chancellor, 29.2.60.
25 Hansard, 4.4.60.
26 BC (60) 03, 3.3.60.
27 NIF (WP) (60) 5 Final.
28 EAS/1/01, 2.6.60.
29 *Ibid.* Copy of 'Note on the Forecast Estimates', 4.7.60.
30 BC 61/01/A. Notes of meetings with Chancellor, 12.9.60, 22.12.60.
31 EAS/1/01. Note of meeting with Chancellor, 14.9.60.
32 *Ibid.* Draft paper for circulation by the Chancellor, 11.11.60.
33 NIF (WP) (60) 7, 12.12.60.
34 NIF (WP) (61) 3 Final, 9.2.61.
35 NIF (WP) (61) 3 Final revised, 9.3.61.
36 BC (M) (60) 6, 22.12.60, and (61) 4, 13.2.61. Sir Frank Lee to Chancellor.
37 BC (61) 04. Notes of meetings with Chancellor, 3 and 27.2.61.
38 BC (M) (61) 9.
39 BC (69) 60.
40 BC (M) (60) 5.
41 BC (M) (61) 1.
42 BC (61) 03A. Note of discussion after dinner between the Chancellor, Lord Robbins, and others, 9.1.61.
43 BC (61) 27.

44 BC (61) 03, 17.3.61.
45 EAS/1/O3A. Rickett to Padmore, 31.5.61.
46 NIF (WP) (61) 6 Final, 14.6.61.
47 BC (62) OIA, 6.6.61.
48 BC (62) O3E, Notes of meetings with the Chancellor, 6 and 15.6.61.
49 2 EAS/1/O3A. Clarke to Padmore, 22.6.61.
50 BC (62) O5E. Sir Norman Brook to Prime Minister, 29.6.61.
51 2 EAS/1/03B. Financial Secretary to Chancellor, 19.7.61.
52 BC (62) O3E. Padmore to Chancellor, 14.7.61.
53 *Ibid.* Note by Mr Cairncross, 18.7.61.
54 *Ibid.* Draft brief by R W B Clarke, 24.7.71.
55 2 EAS/1/04. W Armstrong to Chancellor, 16.5.62.
56 NIF (WP) (62) 9 Final, 15.11.61.
57 BC (61) 35. Note by the Director, Economic Section.
58 BC (61) 41. Sir Frank Lee to Chancellor, 30.11.61.
59 NIF (WP) (62) 2 Final, 20.2.62.
60 BC (M) (62) 8. Sir Frank Lee to Chancellor, 23.2.62.
61 BC (62) 03B. Lord Cromer to Chancellor, 22.1.62.
62 BC (63) 03A. Prime Minister to Chancellor, 11.4.62.
63 NIF (WP) (62) 5 Final, 6.7.62.
64 2 EAS/1/04. Cairncross to Chancellor, 26.6.62.
65 *Ibid.* Note of meeting between Sir Frank Lee, Mr Cairncross, and others.
66 BC (M) (62) 10. Sir Frank Lee to Chancellor.
67 BC (63) 03A. Note of meeting between Sir Frank Lee and others.
68 *Ibid.* Cairncross to Chancellor, 24.10.62.
69 *Ibid.* W Armstrong to Chancellor, 24.10.62.
70 BC (63) 05. Chief Secretary to Chancellor, 10. 12.62.
71 NIF (WP) (62) 11 Final, 3.12.62.
72 BC (62) 43, 3.12.62.
73 BC (62) 49, 10.12.62.
74 2 EAS/1/05, January 1963.
75 NIF (WP) (63) 4 Final, 19.2.63.
76 BC (63) 12 and 15, 15.2.63.
77 BC (63) 19, 16.2.63.
78 BC (63) 03B. Prime Minister to Chancellor, 16.10.62.
79 BC (63) 05.C, December 1962.
80 BC (63) 05C, 11.1.63.
81 Hansard, 4.4.63.
82 NIF (WP) (63) 14 Final, 10.7.63.
83 2 EAS/1/05. Cairncross to W Armstrong, for Chancellor, 25.10.63.
84 NIF (WP) (63) 17 Final, 13.11.63, BC (63) 37. See an interesting note, 'Historical Memorandum on Reflation and Modernisation, 1962–63', prepared by Mr Wiggins in November 1964. This analyses the interaction of the 'Modernisation of Britain' ideas, launched by the Prime Minister in October 1962, with the measures of reflation. (2 EAS 1/06 and PIO files.)
85 2 EAS/1/06. Hopkin to Mitchell, for Chancellor, 18.12.63.

86 2 EAS/1/06. Cairncross to Chancellor, January 1964.
87 BC (64) 03 Pt 9, 14.1.64.
88 BC (64) 5 and BC minutes, 31.1.64.
89 NIF (WP) (64) 2 Final, 11.2.64.
90 BC minutes 17.2.64 and BC (M) (64) 3.
91 EP (64) 65, 20.3.64.
92 Hansard, 24.4.64.
93 2 EAS/1/06, Cairncross to Chancellor, 4.6.64.
94 NIF (WP) (64) 8 Final, 1.7.64.
95 2 EAS/1/06. 'Views of the Clearing Banks', 9.7.64.
96 BC (64) 21.
97 BC (M) (64) 4.
98 2 EAS/1/06. Cairncross to Chancellor, 13 and 23.7.64.
99 *Ibid*. Cairncross for Chancellor, 18.9.64.
100 GB (64) 46 addendum, 23.10.64.
101 2 EAS/1/06. Cairncross to Armstrong, 30.11.64.

Control of demand in relation to wages and prices

At the beginning of this period the restoration and maintenance of a stable price level was one of the chief avowed objects of Government policy. Later, from 1962 onwards, this objective was less often paraded; but the official incomes policy of the 'pause' and the 'guiding light' aimed at restraining the rate of increase of wages and salaries to something near the rate of growth of productivity. This, it was thought, would stabilise unit costs of production and so remove the main cause of rising prices. It might have been expected that control of demand would have been used, deliberately and continuously, as a principal means of achieving these objectives.

In fact, the files show clearly that control of demand was *not* so used for this purpose; nor, apparently, was reliance on it as the *principal* instrument ever even contemplated. No official or Minister, so far as can be seen, ever asked the rude questions: by how much would total demand have to be reduced to keep prices stable; or, later, by how much would it have to be cut back in monetary terms to offset the effects on prices of excessive wage increases, and what would happen to production and unemployment if it were so cut.

This is, of course, not to deny that the Government's price and wage objectives were frequently, indeed usually, in mind when decisions were taken about the restriction or expansion of demand. Fear of upsetting them probably delayed the beginning of reflation in 1958 by three or four months, and later they were many times used as a reason for caution in expansion or as a supporting argument for restriction of demand. Mr Selwyn Lloyd's 'package' of July 1961 was, indeed, forced by a crisis of sterling; but the argument that restriction of demand would reinforce the direct attempt to check wage increases by the 'pay pause' was freely used by officials. Sir William Armstrong's warning to Mr Maudling in February 1964,[1] that a fall in unemployment below 1.7 per cent would be accompanied by a rapid further rise in wage costs, has already been quoted. It was not challenged, at a time when the 'guiding light' itself was flickering to extinction, but was accepted as a decisive reason for trying to prevent a fall to this level.

The positive thinking behind this attitude was fairly simple. Sir Robert Hall several times argued that low unemployment encouraged trade unions and shop stewards to press for larger wage increases and that high demand made employers less unwilling to grant them: as an additional cost common to everybody, they could in conditions of high demand, easily be passed on (except in export markets) in higher prices. But he never maintained that, in the absence of high demand, there would be no excessive wage increases and no price increases. Moreover, in December 1958, when there was some slack in the economy, his advice was that Budget concessions designed to lower prices and reduce income tax on the lower incomes would do more for moderation in wage demands than the maintenance of high unemployment (the figure was then about 2.5 per cent).[2] He generally emphasised increases in the cost of living as a force behind the pressure for wage increases. Thus in February 1961 he wrote:

There are some signs that we may be returning to the condition where the rate of rise of consumer prices is itself a powerful force making for wage increases, and thus to a wages/prices spiral.[3]

There was little or no suggestion, in these years, that the levels of demand reached had much effect in pulling prices up directly. The emphasis was all on the push from the cost side, modified by the varying but generally inadequate ability of employers to absorb it by greater efficiency. More positively, Sir Robert Hall was the chief champion within the Treasury of a direct attack on the wage/price problem by means of Government guidance as to the general levels of wage increases which could be afforded in the national interest. In May 1958 he advised it as the proper accompaniment of reflation;[4] but when this advice was rejected, he did not suggest that reflation should stop.

Mr Cairncross on the whole took much the same view as his predecessor about the relation of control of demand to the wages problem, though he added some variants and probably had less faith in the effectiveness of a Government-guided incomes policy.[5] He was interested in the question of 'wage drift': that is, the tendency for actual earnings per person employed to increase, in most years, faster than the negotiated rates of wages. He was at first inclined to attribute this to 'demand pull' from employers bidding competitively for labour in times of high demand. Wage drift was certainly larger then. However, an inquiry by the Economic Section, though inconclusive, suggested that much of it was due to the working of more overtime after negotiated agreements for shorter hours or otherwise, or to local factory floor bargains; this was consistent with the 'cost-push' rather than the 'demand pull' idea. From 1963 onwards Mr Cairncross also sometimes rather discounted the old argument that wage increases must be restrained in the interests of the balance of payments, pointing out that cost and price inflation in Europe, and perhaps also in the United States, was catching up with that in Britain.

The actual course of events seems to support the view that variations in general demand, exercised alternately a restraining and a stimulating effect on the wage increases, but that excess demand was not itself the cause of them. Wage increases went on throughout the period at rates which were always, except in 1959, greater than the growth of average productivity. But the rates of increase did differ very markedly in a somewhat lagged relationship with the movements of general demand and industrial activity. Thus the annual rate of increase in hourly wage rates, which had been 7 per cent in the later stages of the boom from January 1956 to June 1957, dropped to half that rate in the recession to December 1958, and still further, to 1.2 per cent, in 1959 in the early stage of the upswing. The year 1960, however, showed a jump of 6.7 per cent, and the rise continued at around 6 per cent a year until checked by the 'wage pause' in the summer of 1961, the flattening out of demand in the following 12 months and the recession of the autumn of 1962. Increases during the reflation of 1963 were at only 3.25 per cent a year in the first half, but accelerated later, to 5 per cent in 1964 and 6.75 per cent in 1965. Since unemployment also lagged behind the movements of production and general demand, there was a close inverse relation in time between the percentage of unemployment and the pace of wage increases. But at the highest levels of unemployment in this period, about 2.5 per cent, wage increases still went on.

These relationships do not prove that restriction of demand, if continued long enough, could not have kept average wage increases within the limits of the average growth of productivity. If, for instance, there had been no reflation of demand in 1958, or a much smaller one, it seems likely that wage increases in 1960 would have followed the pattern of those in 1959, which were within these limits. Again, if there had been less haste to reflate in order to check the industrial recession of the autumn of 1962, or stronger restraining action in July 1961, it is possible that the 2.5 per cent 'guiding light' might have been made effective in 1963 and 1964. But there is no reason to suppose that this would have removed the underlying pressures for excessive increases whenever opportunity offered. It looks as if denial of such opportunity would have required the maintenance of an unemployment rate of at least 2.5 per cent, as well as entailing some postponement of the recovery of industrial investment in late 1959 and late 1963. This would have meant an under-use of national resources which, in the political circumstances, was probably intolerable. It was, after all, the CBI as well as the TUC which championed expansion as the cure, and the Treasury economists themselves seem to have measured excessive pressure of demand in terms of unemployment at 1.75 per cent (around 420,000 in the United Kingdom), rather than 2.5 per cent (around 600,000). In November 1961 Mr Cairncross put it even lower; 'excess demand begins to appear once the level of unemployment falls below the number of unfilled vacancies. This usually occurs around 1.5 per cent, but sometimes less.'*

Though the matter does not seem to have been systematically set out, there were probably reasons inherent in the Treasury's general approach to control of demand, and in the forecasting methods on which it was based, which would have made it difficult, indeed unnatural, to regard it as the primary instrument for dealing with cost and price inflation. Its basic purpose was conceived in terms of securing a proper balance between total demands and supplies of goods and services, expressed in *real*, not *monetary*, terms. Such a balance was not necessarily inconsistent with a progressive rise in money costs and prices. Thus, to take an over-simplified illustration, if in any period demand in monetary terms was expected to increase by a given amount, and costs and prices of output *by the same amount*, the initial degree of pressure on real resources would remain unchanged; and, if the initial balance were thought to be right, no stimulatory or restrictive action would seem called for to improve it. And the end-product of the forecasts was always expressed in terms of constant prices – 1954 prices until February 1962, 1958 prices thereafter. This disguised both the amount of price inflation expected in the forecast period (though this was always stated in the text of the report) as well as that which had taken place over several past years. Of course, in order to arrive at these 'real terms' results, the forecasters had to make most of their calculations of the growth of incomes,

* This intersection occurred at 1.4 per cent in March 1961, and continued until October, but not again until 1965.

etc., in current monetary terms. But, for this purpose, they took as *given* an expected rate
of wage and salary increases, derived from recent trends, modified after 1961 by allowance
for the effects of the 'pause and the 'guiding light' The resultant income levels were then
expressed in 'real' terms. Similarly, for prices they forecast rates of increase which were
mainly derived from expected movements of import prices, home unit costs of production,
and known changes in indirect taxation, with some allowance for time-lag. But, for the
valuation of output and its expected changes, these were also deflated to a constant price
basis. The final focus of the forecasts was thus always an expected rate of change in the
gross domestic product, valued at constant prices and compared with the resources of
labour, capacity, and improved productivity which were expected to be available to meet
it. The implication was that any Government action to control demand would be directed
primarily to improving the relationship between physical magnitudes – real consumption
and investment, production, real resources, especially of labour.

It was not the forecasters' business to say what would happen if control of demand were
to be mainly directed to securing a different objective, such as stability of prices or a
particular average rate of wage increases. They were not asked that question. It is,
however, in retrospect remarkable that nobody else was asked to set possible answers to
it in any systematic way. The point may be exemplified. In 1963, in order to stimulate the
economy, the Government made Budgetary concessions which were expected to add
about £270 million to disposable money incomes, as well as taking other measures to
increase spending. Yet at the same time its incomes policy prescribed increases in wages
and salaries not to exceed 2.5/3.5 per cent per head, which would have added about
£260/£360 million, to personal disposable income (after taxation etc.). In principle, being
offset by greater productivity, such an increase in earnings per head should not have raised
costs or prices. In the event, average earnings rose by over 7 per cent in 1963/64, thus
doubling the 'permissible' increase in total disposable incomes from that source and
forcing up unit costs of production by around 4 per cent. There was indeed, during 1963
an increase of about 6 per cent in the money value of the total domestic expenditure (some
£1,800 million); but about a quarter of this represented a fall in the value of money which
it was one of the Government's objects to prevent. Few people believed at the time that
the degree of wage restraint assumed by the forecasters and prescribed by Government
policy could be achieved easily, if at all. Clearly, if this objective had been given deliberate
priority, the Budgetary treatment would have been different. But how much difference
would have been needed, and with what other effects on the economy?

A closely related question is that of the direct effect of excessive wage and salary
increases on the balance of demand and supply in real terms. This deserves more explicit
analysis than it seems to have received within the Treasury in this period. As has been
said, the forecasters incorporated allowances for these increases in their calculations of
total *money* income, and a number of scattered references suggest that they thought that
big wage increases helped to maintain or to push up the level of demand in *real* terms –

i.e. after allowing for cost and price increases within the same period. But I have not seen any precise discussion of how this worked out as a stimulus to the economy generally.

Wage increases raise the money incomes of the recipients but simultaneously affect unit costs of production. If they are greater than the increase of productivity they must also either raise prices or result in an offsetting reduction of incomes from profits. But a large part – in this period probably between a quarter and a third – of total wage and increases are automatically removed from incomes by income tax and surtax; and, in addition, the forecasters, who devoted much attention to the subject, found that a surprisingly high proportion of the marginal increments of incomes were saved: they put this at 20 per cent during the years 1957-63, 'with a tendency for it to be high when real personal income is rising fast, and vice versa'. Thus the addition made by wage and salary increases to consumers' demand in money terms is much less than the amount of the wage increases themselves and, if the accompanying improvement in productivity is small, it may be less than the total net additions to costs and, in the end, to prices. In so far as such net additions to costs are in fact passed on in higher prices within the period, consumers' demand in real terms may fall rather than rise, and thus check the growth of production. In so far as they are not so passed on, profitability will be reduced and production may be discouraged by this as well as, later on, by a fall in spending from profit incomes. It is not possible to see from the NIF reports whether these considerations affected their forecasts of the growth of demand and production in real terms; or, if they did, what magnitudes were involved. Though wage and salary increases went on all through this period, they were very much bigger in the later stages of the two upswings and early in the recessions than at other times, as 1960 and the first half of 1961 and again in 1964. It may well be that a process such as is outlined above may have had something to do with the hesitancy both of production and of demand in real terms (e.g. in the volume of retail sales) which surprised the forecasters in 1962 and 1964. Presumably the effect would be greater if the disparity between wage increases and the growth of productivity were larger, and the impact on prices quicker, as has happened in 1969 and 1970.

Credit policy was used, as has been shown, throughout the period as the servant and one of the chief instruments of the policy of control of domestic demand; and the Government's control over the banking system, exercised through the Bank of England, became more extensive and more refined with the new device of 'special deposits' and with the reintroduction and development of the directives to the banks about the priorities to be observed in their advances. Bank rate was used in its traditional role as a regulator of the external demand for sterling, but became less important for that purpose as the Bank came to rely more on its arrangements with other central banks and with the IMF for dealing with short-term variations. Its movements, or the absence of them, thus became more closely related to the control of internal demand, though there were still times when the external and internal considerations conflicted. But there is no sign of any desire, either by the Treasury or the Bank, to make credit policy or control of the total money supply bite directly to check wage and salary increases or the rise of prices, by keeping business short of cash. The directives on bank lending probably helped to channel a lion's share of advances, within a sometimes restricted total, to direct employers of labour, rather than to borrowers for consumption. There was little sign during this period that many employers were deterred from agreeing to wage increases by actual shortage of cash or of bank credit.

As regards prices, no one seems to have advocated an attempt to set pre-determined ceilings to the growth of money supply which would be sufficient to support the present level of prices but no more. It is highly uncertain whether such an aim could have been made effective had it been tried; what is certain is that any attempt to apply it would soon have conflicted with requirements for expansion of credit derived from a policy to expand demand and make fuller use of resources. The Bank of England, formally at least, washed its hands of the matter: it repeatedly said that, though excessive wage increases were no doubt bad and dangerous, the main cause of credit inflation was excessive public expenditure financed by excessive borrowing, which made its control of credit and the money supply very difficult in any case. Within the Treasury, the Economic Section had a deep-rooted distrust of crude quantity theories of money and would probably have rejected as impracticable any attempt to relate directly increases in the price level to defined increases in the supply of money. They may well have been right. It is an interesting fact that during this period the total money supply, as indicated by the amounts of currency with the public plus deposits with domestic banks, accepting houses, and overseas banks, did *not* increase nearly as fast as the gross national income at current prices, and grew not much faster than the gross national product valued in terms of 1958 prices.* Presumably, therefore, to maintain the 1958 level of prices throughout until 1964 would have required stability in the total money supply, despite a growth of national product of over a quarter in real terms – if, indeed, such a growth could have taken place at all in those monetary circumstances.

Notes

1   BC (M) (64) 2, 20.4.64.
2   BC (59) 03. Hall to Padmore, 17.12.58.
3   BC (61) 3, 9.2.61.
4   BC 59/03A. Hall to Makins, 16.7.58.
5   e.g. 2 EAS/1/03A. 'Treasury Doctrine', 29.11.61.

---

*   The figures are: increases 1964 over 1958: money supply, 30.7 per cent; gross national product at current prices, 42.7 per cent; gross national product at constant (1958) prices, 25.8 per cent. The rise in unit costs of home production was 12.7 per cent, that in the retail price index about 16. per cent.

A Review of the Forecasts

Gross Domestic Product*

Forecasts of the movements of the gross national product and of its main components must obviously be the basis for any attempt to control the course of the economy. They are equally obviously, in the present state of kuowledge, uncertain and liable to be wrong. The margins concerned in the period under consideration were narrow. A rise of less than 2 per cent in GDP in a year (involving quarterly changes of only about £84 million at 1954 prices at the beginning and £135 million at 1958 prices at the end) meant a substantial reduction of pressure on resources and rising unemployment; a rise of more than 4 per cent meant a growing pressure which could not be sustained for long. And the total change in GDP was a summation of changes in the main components, sometimes offsetting, sometimes reinforcing each other, which could be individually larger than the total change.

No one realised the uncertainty more than the Treasury forecasters themselves. There is no dogmatic tone in their reports, and they conducted several revealing post mortems. They were debarred from forecasting within a range and, usually, from showing the effect on their results of varying some of the assumptions they had adopted; this would, indeed, have made both the work and its presentation very complicated. It is, however, a fair point of criticism that the policy makers too often adopted the forecasts as a basis for recommended action without fully assessing their uncertainty and without considering other plans in case they should be wrong.

Throughout this period forecasting the internal situation was the business of the National Incomes Forecasts Working Party (NIF), while forecasting external development was in the hand. of the Balance of Payments Working Party (BP). Both had Treasury chairmen and secretaries, but they drew heavily on information and judgements provided by other departments which were represented on them, notably the Central Statistical Office, Board of Trade, Ministry of Labour, and the Bank of England. These departments between them also assembled and published most of the statistical series (employment, unemployment, unfilled vacancies, exports and imports, volume and value of retail sales, bank advances, etc.) which provided the basis for the forecasters' assessment of the current state and recent trend of the economy. They also conducted some regular forward-looking inquiries, such as that of the Board of Trade into investment intentions in industry. Generally, the NIF Working Party used forecasts of exports arrived at by the BP Working Party, and vice versa for forecasts of imports; but occasionally there were differences of opinion which had to be resolved by informal consultation. In 1961 the February forecast of internal growth was revised upwards within a month to take account of a higher export

---

*   Gross Domestic Product differs from Gross National Product by the omission of net property income from abroad. This was during this period about 1.4 per cent of Gross National Product.

forecast provided by the BP Working Party: this, as turned out, was very far from justified. On the other hand, failure to foresee the scale of the rise in imports in 1960 and again in 1964 upset the forecasts of the balance of payments for these years.

The NIF Working Party made three reports each year – in November or early December, early February, and June, with minor variations of timing. The first two were geared to preparations for the Budget, and the June Report reassessed the situation in the light of Budget changes and could bear on policy decisions to be taken before the recess. The December Report had the longest period available for its preparation. But, as appeared in several years, the late autumn was an awkward period for judging the state and trends of the economy because much of the information necessary for assessing changes after the summer holidays was not yet available; and, the tone of a forecast having been set in November/December, it seems to have been difficult to alter it radically in January/February even with the help of fresh information. The period covered by the forecasts was gradually lengthened. Those made in December 1958 and in February and June 1959 dealt with 1959 only, and those in December 1959 and February 1960 with 1960. But the report of June 1960 looked ahead for 12 months from that time, and that of June 1961 did the same. In the forecast of July 1962 figures were given up to the end of 1963, though it was focussed on changes between the first quarter of 1962 and the third quarter of 1963; and the July forecasts of 1963 and 1964 both looked forward 18 months to the end of 1964 and 1965 respectively. The December and February forecast periods were also somewhat extended, though their main focus was on the next financial year. This lengthening of the period of forecasts reflected a recognition that some stimuli and deterrents, particularly to investment, took a long time to work through. It was also necessary for the policy of gradually slowing down the growth of the economy to a sustainable rate as the slack of 1962 and 1963 was progressively taken up. Though figures were tabulated for each quarter, at 1954 prices until the report of Februay 1962 and, at 1958 prices thereafter, most of the discussion was in terms of percentage changes in real terms over a twelve-month period, with often a judgement about the annual rate of change in the last quarter covered by the forecasts. This method placed great weight on the assessment of both the level and the trend of activity at the starting point of the forecasts. Pressure of demand was measured mainly by the changes in the amount or percentage of unemployment which were expected to accompany the forecast changes in GDP, though the forecasters emphasised that the relationship was sometimes erratic. Reference was also sometimes made to actual or expected bottlenecks in particular sectors, especially construction and engineering, as being likely to 'frustrate' demand and to hold back the actual growth of GDP in real terms.

Between the formal forecasts a close watch was kept on the main monthly indicators. From 1962 onwards charts of these were given a fairly wide circulation in the Treasury, and the practise developed whereby the Economic Adviser gave the Chancellor an appraisal of the situation each month: this was often circulated to other Ministers in the Economic Policy Comittee. For most of the indicators, however, changes over one or two months were highly erratic and difficult to interpret, and the wisdcm of basing policy changes upon them was doubtful. Nonetheless, they certainly influenced the decision to begin reflation in the autumn of 1962, for which the June forecast provided no basis; and they brought an earlier realisation than could be obtained from the forecast of the pace which that reflation had acquired a year later. In the sumer of 1964 conclusions drawn from them were probably misleadingly optimistic.

In making the forecasts themselves there were two closely related problems – the assesment of the state and trend of the economy at the time of the report or shortly before it, and the making of the forecasts for the future. These, though they could draw on some forward information about, for example, industry's investment plans and provisions for Government expenditure, were necessarily largely a projection of what were believed to be the current trends from the current level. Misjudgement of the current situation could therefore affect the forecasts in two ways. If the current trend either of the gross national product as a whole, or of one of its volatile components, such as stock-building or industrial investment, were wrongly judged, the forecasts a year ahead were likely to be much too high or too low. Second, even if the trend were rightly judged an incorrect assessment of the starting level could falsify conclusions about the amount of slack likely to be left in the economy during the forecast period. Independent changes beginning within the period could of course also affect the result. All forecasts were made on the assumption that Government fiscal, credit and wages policies remained unchanged; when changes did in fact take place, their effects were estimated and the result incorporated, along with a later assessment of other developments, in the next forecast.

The NIF reports and forecasts were written almost entirely in terms of seasonally adjusted quarterly figures, except occasionally when unemployment was under discussion. Seasonal adjustment of the actual figures was necessary for the establishment of any trend. But, as may be seen from the chart VII, the variations in the actual figures of GDP from quarter to quarter were both irregular from year to year and very large indeed – much larger in fact than the effect of any 'trend' of activity within them. For example, the *average* fall of GNP (at 1958 prices) from the fourth quarter to the succeeding first quarter was 4.8 per cent, with a maximum of 6.4 per cent in 1961/62; and a minimum of 3.6 per cent in 1958/9; whereas the seasonally corrected series, finalised only long after the event, showed a rise of 1.7 per cent in 1958/59 and of smaller amounts in two other years, and small falls in the remaining three. It is clear that the need to make seasonal adjustments could easily cause the level of GNP for a recent quarter to be placed as much as 1 per cent or 2 per cent too high or too low, with resultant misinterpretation of both the current level and trend on which the forecast for the future had to be based. There was the further trouble that Ministers and the public was more impressed by actualities than by trends; the spectre of 'winter unemployment' in particular was always with them. The extreme case was provided by the hard winter of 1962/63: the total of registered unemployed in Great Britain jumped from 525,000 (2.2 per cent) in the fourth quarter of 1962 to 800,000 (3.6 per cent) in the first quarter of 1963, although the level of GNP, *seasonally corrected*, later showed a fall of less than 0.5 per cent. Zeal for a reflationary Budget in April was bound to be considerable, whatever the forecasters might say – and in fact they too over-estimated the need for stimulus to the economy.

There are many difficulties in comparing the forecasts with the actual outturn on a quarterly basis throughout the period. The two main methods of calculating the gross domestic product – from the expenditure side and the output side – often gave significantly different results, particularly from one quarter to another; and some use was made of a third method – deflation of income statistics by a price index. Measurement first in terms of prices and production weights of 1954 and later of 1958 caused discrepancies, especially at the time of changeover; this was applied to the CSO series from the third quarter of 1961 but to the NIF forecasts only from July 1962

Fresh information and successive revisions of old information were incorporated in the CSO series for many years after the event. The NIF forecasts did not use precisely the CSO definitions and coverage, and differed in themselves from time to time both in form and in their use of seasonal and other smoothing devices. Nevertheless, since a standard of reference is essential for appraisal, in the following table the Treasury forecasts are compared with the series of quarterly figures published by the CSO in *Economic Trends* for October 1966, the results obtained from expenditure and from output being averaged. These are probably the best approximation available to the actual course of GDP in the period. It must, however, be noted that successive revisions before that have not only altered the shape of the curve of GDP in some years, but have also generally raised its level. This is one of the reasons why the NIF forecast figures usually ran well below the levels of outturn which were finally recorded. This does not necessarily mean that they underestimated the pressure of demand; rather, that the whole contemporary picture of demand and production was stated in somewhat lower terms.

In considering the validity of the forecasts, it must of course be remembered that they were all made on the assumption that Govornment fiscal and credit policy remained unchanged. When substantial changes were in fact made after the forecasts, some part of the divergence between forecasts and outturns can usually be traced to them; in other cases they validated forecasts which, on their own assumptions, would have been wrong. But, when allowance is made for this, it appears that the forecasts were badly wrong for 1959, 1962 and 1963; while for the first half of 1961, though the growth predicted was not much too high, it was projected from too low a base and thus misjudged the amount of pressure on resources involved.

In the report of December 1958, apparently because of erratic figures for imports and for reduction of stock, it was not realised that an u-turn had already started in the last quarter of the year. Therefore, despite the reflation already begun by the Government, a very sharp fall in GDP was forecast for the first quarter of 1959, with recovery later to a level little above that of 1958. .The February report only amended this to allow for a larger rise in the last quarter. Even the June report, which estimated that the Budget concessions would add £150 million to demand within the calendar year, only put GDP in the last quarter some 4 to 5 per cent above a year earlier. In fact GDP rose very fast throughout the year and by the fourth quarter was nearly 7 per cent above that of the same period of 1958. Reasons for this misjudgment of the pace of growth in 1959 have already been discussed (pp.36-39). Its consequences were serious. An expansionary budget in 1959 was probably economically sensible as well as politically unavoidable. But the extent of the concessions might have been much smaller, and the troubles of 1960 and 1961 probably less, if the momentum of the recovery which was already in progress had been rightly judged.

Gross Domestic Product: forecast and actual growth

Date of report	Period covered	Percentage change	
		Forecast growth	Actual growth
12.12.58	1958-59	1%	4%
	1958 IV-1959 IV	1.5%	7%
25.2.59	1958-59	1.5%	as above
	1958 IV-1959 IV	2%	
28.5.59	1958-59	3.5%	as above
	1958 IV-1959 IV	4%/5%	
10.12.59	1959 IV to 1960 IV	3.5%/3.8%	3%
9.2.60	1959 IV to 1960 IV	5.5%	3%
12.5.60	1960 1st half to 1961 1st half	2.5% (pressure of demand expected to be slightly lowered)	3%
12.12.60	1960 III-1961 III	Very small - about 1%	3%
9.3.61	1960 IV-1961 IV	2.75%	1.75%
14.6.61	1961 1st half to 1962 1st half	3.5%-3.75% in all	1% in all
15.11.61	1961 IV-1963 I	Annual rate 3%-3.75% in all	1% in all
20.2.62	1962 I-1963 I	nearly 5%	1%
6.7.62	1962 I-1963 I	4.25%	1%
	1963 I-1963 III	annual rate 3.25%-1.6% in all	5%
30.11.62	1962 III-1963 III	nearly 3%	4%
19.2.63	1963 I-1964 I	?3.25% - may start rising early in 1963 1st half	8.6%
10.7.63	1963 II-1964 IV	Annual rate 6%-8% in all	8% in all
13.11.63	1963 II-1964 IV	Annual rate 5.75% - total 7.1% (faster at first, 5.5% 1964)	8% in all 1963 II/IV4% 1963 IV/64 IV4%
11.2.64	1963 III-1965 I	Annual rate near 6%-9% in all	7.5% in all
1.7.64	1963 1st half to 1964 1st half; 1964 1st half to 1965 1st half; 1965 II/1965 IV	6% 4% Annual rate 3.25%-1.6% in all	7.25% 3.0% 1.9% in all

In December 1959 the extent and force of the boom was still not recognised, so that in the first forecast for 1960 the starting point of GDP in the fourth quarter of 1959 was placed about 4 per cent (£160 million at 1954 prices) too low. From this the moderate and steady growth of about 3.5 per cent expected during 1960 was not thought likely to strain the economy. As has been noticed, this forecast was revised after Christmas 1959 under pressure of alarm at the pace of expansion which was actually taking place. The February forecast placed the level of GDP at the end of 1959 much higher (though probably still not high enough). It then allowed for a further steep rise in the first half of 1960, but forecast little growth thereafter. In the event, the position at the end of the year was very close to this second forecast; but this result was largely fortuitous. The rapid rise of production and GNP ended with the first quarter, and the subsequent flattening and slight decline was no doubt accentuated if not wholly caused by the credit and other restrictions imposed at the end of April.

The first forecast for 1961 was made in May 1960, just after these restrictive measures had been taken. It was for steady growth at 2.5 per cent from mid-1960 to mid-1961. In fact the rapid rise of GNP had already stopped and it remained sluggish until the end of 1960. This check was exaggerated in the assessments made in both December 1960 and in February 1961, so that the starting level for 1961 was placed too low. The forecasters saw no strong expansionary forces at work, and expected some decline in the rate of growth of stocks. They therefore predicted only a small rise of GDP, of around 1 per cent, in the first half of the year, with decline or stability thereafter, and a substantial decline in the pressure on labour. These forecasts gave no warning of the pressure which actually developed during the first and second quarters and which helped to precipitate Mr Selwyn Lloyd's July measures. However, as has been noted (p. 22), senior officials thought that this pressure was already excessive and pressed for stronger action to restrain demand than the Chancellor was prepared to take in the Budget. The June forecast did not register most of the build-up which had already taken place, but predicted very rapid growth and rising pressure on resources for the rest of the year and in the first half of 1962. This was the basis for officials' calculations of the amount of restraint required in the July measures and, though these were not as severe as officials advised, they thoroughly vitiated the forecast.

The failure of the forecasters to predict the onset of a recession in the second half of 1962 has probably received more outside criticism than any other mistake during the period. In November 1961 they rather minimised the immediate effects of the July measures and expected a fairly steady growth of 3.25 per cent in GDP from the fourth quarter of 1961 to the fourth quarter of 1962, continuing into 1963. In February 1962, they recognised that the setback after July had been substantial, but forecast even faster growth, over 4 per cent, from a lower base; and 4 per cent growth was announced as the target for 1962 in the Budget speech. Even in July, when little of the growth seemed yet to have taken place, they still expected some rise later in the year, accelerating in 1963. But for all of these forecasts the base used in 1961 seems to have been too low, Throughout, the forecasters were acutely aware that the boom in industrial investment was past its peak and that a very substantial fall in it must be allowed for. They thought, however, that this would be more tha offset by the growth of public and other private investment. In the event, the outturn figures show that manufacturing investment was some £170 million lower in the last quarter of 1962 than a year earlier, and that this was not quite offset by the rise in other categories of fixed investment. In any case the dynamic provided in 1959, 1960 and 1961 by the growth of fixed investment by about £100 million a year was absent in 1962; and the outturn figures for GDP, though showing erratic quarterly movements, gave a growth between the last quarters of 1961 and 1962 of only about 1 per cent, instead of the 4 per cent which was expected. Unemployment, instead of growing slightly at the beginning of 1962 and then remaining about constant at about 1.8 per cent, as had been originally expected, rose steeply in the last half of the year and reached nearly 2.5 per cent (600,000) by December. This was especially embarrassing because, as late as July, the Working Party had been asked at the instigation of the Minister of Labour to examine precisely this possibility and had dimissed it with scorn. Their own estimate for December was then 475,000.

The NIF Working Party were asked to hold a post mortem on the forecasts made in 1962. This was completed in May 1963. By then the general course of events in 1962 was fairly clear, although the outturn figures which they used differ considerably from the later figures quoted above. They concentrated mainly on the February forecast, which was the most expansionist and which preceded the budget. They found that the main cause of the error was that exports and private investment together were forecast £500 million too high, with a consequential overstatement of consumption by £150/£200 million. This total of £650/£700 million accounted for 2/2.25 per cent of the forecast rise of 4 per cent in GDP between the fourth quarters of 1961 and 1962; the actual growth they thought was 'of the order of 1 per cent'. (The report does not explain the remaining discrepancy of 0.75–1 per cent.) The export forecast, taken over from the BP Working Party and coloured by an optimistic view of world trade and by the expectation that we should succeed in joining the European Economic Community, had been for a rise of 7.75 per cent in real terms during 1962. In the event exports rose only in the first half, and in the fourth quarter were only 2 per cent more than a year earlier. This shortfall reduced final demand by 1 per cent, apart from consequentials. For private investment, the level at the end of 1961 had been overstated and the fall during the year under-estimated, mainly because manufacturing investment fell by nearly twice as much as had been expected, and investment in distribution and other categories also fell instead of rising. As a result, total fixed investment was running in the fourth quarter of 1962 at an annual rate £200 million below the forecast. These errors were attributed to the lack of firm information about actual private investment later than to the third quarter of 1961, and to reliance on the Board of Trade's second 'investment intentions' inquiry, made at the end of the year. This had suggested that manufacturing investment would fall by only 1 per cent, and investment in distribution rise by 8 per cent, up to the middle of 1962. In fact both of them declined in that period, and the trend projected for the rest of the year had been much too high. The error in the forecast of personal consumption was mainly a consequence of these shortfalls; but it was admitted that, in addition, the effect of price increases, especially by nationalised industries, had been understated and the amount of borrowing for hire-purchase over-estimated. Unemployment had been forecast by using a formula based, after allowance for time-lags, on the ratio between changes in expected output and 'potential' output (these included both improvements in productivity and additions to the labour force). Growth of potential output was put at a 3.25 per cent year during 1961 and 1962; a 1 per cent change in this ratio was thought to go with a change of 45,000–50,000 in unemployment (about 0.2 per cent). Thus the forecast growth of 4 per cent in GDP should have gone with a small fall in unemployment, and the actual growth of about 1 per cent with a rise of 135,000–150,000. The actual growth of unemployment (177,000 in Great Britain from December 1961 to December 1962) was rather more than this, for reasons which this report did not try to explain. It is clear that the movements of unemployment in relation to those of GDP were erratic in other years also, even as late as July 1964 the NIF report said that the relationship was not fully understood and put forward an estimate only with reserve.

The report added that the July and November forecasts continued to give too optimistic a picture. That of July still put exports and investments too high, and was also too hopeful on stock-building and on hire-purchase, which did not respond as expected to the relaxation of restrictions in May. The November report failed on current diagnosis. Too much reliance was placed on a good index of production figure in September; too little on signs of falling business confidence and on rising unemployment. The level of GDP in the fourth quarter of 1962 was therefore placed too high. This comment is correct. But it was written before the main fault of the November 1962 forecast was realised, that it greatly understated the pace of recovery even after the further stimulus given by the budget of 1963. For further discussion, see below.

The report indicated several points for possible improvement in future. It emphasised the critical importance of the export forecast both in its own right and as an accelerator and multiplier. It discussed the difficulties of relying on the 'intentions survey' for private manufacturing investment, but could see no obvious remedy. It suggested that some way should be found of giving more weight to 'qualitative' information about the state of business confidence, and the desirability of using and comenting on other contemporary appraisals, such as those made with growing authority by the NIESR. It also proposed more work, which was later done by the CSO, on the technical methods of collecting and using information about the industrial sector. Though the forecasts and the reports on them did thereafter become fuller and more refined in detail, no radical changes of approach seem to have been suggested or made.

For 1963 the report of November 1962, taking account of the reflationary measures which had already been announced, foresaw a steady growth of about 3 per cent in GDP between the third quarters of 1963 and 1964. The February report lowered the base point sharply (and rather too much) to allow more for the set-back of 1962, and stressed the amount of slack in the economy. It predicted that, after a slow start, GDP might grow at to the last quarter of 1964 personal consumption, stimulated by the Government's measures, would make the running at first, with stock-building and fixed investment replacing it as the dynamic later. In July, higher figures were used for the first half of the year, and the growth rate was stepped up sharply in the second half to take account of the expansionary budget. But even so growth between the fourth quarters of 1962 and 1963 was shown at only 5 per cent, and at 5.5–6 per cent between the second quarters of 1963 and 1964. In the event, GDP grew by over 7 per cent in the first period, slackening to about 6.25 per cent in the second, but reaching a level at the end of it much above that forecast for it even in July 1963.

Failure to foresee the scale and pace of expansion in 1963, and failure to recognise it quickly enough, led to many of the troubles of 1964. But the reasons for this enormous and sudden change in the economic climate after the gloom of 1962 are still mysterious. Manufacturing investment went on falling almost to the end of 1963, and so did total fixed investment until the second quarter; so the dynamic was not here. Exports picked up smartly from the beginning of the year, and the increase in orders and work on them must have begun earlier; and the total growth of exports in 1963, at around £300 million, was more than double that 1962. But it accounted directly for less than a quarter of the total growth of GDP. Many of the Government's reflationary measures which were announced before the end of 1962 can have directly increased spending only late in 1963. Others, such as the cuts in purchase tax, should have had earlier effect; but in fact little rise in consumers' expenditure (in real terms) was recorded before the second quarter, and in the event it was little higher than six months earlier. There is no evidence of heavy stock-building early in the year. It does, however, seem likely that the change in Government policy in the autumn had widespread effects on business confidence, and that these were already becoming cumulative in the first quarter of 1963. Others, such as the cuts in purchase tax, should have had earlier effect; but in fact little rise in consumers' expenditure (in real terms) was recorded before the second quarter. Stocks were further depleted in the first quarter. It does, however, seem likely that the change in Government policy in the autumn had widespread effects on business confidence, and that these were already becoming cumulative in the first quarter of 1963, despite the setback to production caused by the hard winter. Thereafter, the big further stimulus given by the Budget and by rising public expenditure accelerated and exaggerated an expansion which was already well begun and having its own interacting effects on demand and production. As had happened in 1959, weakness in the forecasting led to an excessive budgetary stimulus.

The forecasts of November 1963 and of February and July 1964 were probably the most successful in the period in predicting the rate of growth of GNP, though they all probably rather under-estimated the level which it had already reached at the end of 1963. It must, however, be said that their success owed something to the mild restraint imposed by the Budget of 1964, after the first two of them were made; and it is also true that the actual demand in 1964 was sufficient to absorb not merely the forecast increase in production but also an unforeseen volume of imports – with serious effects for the balance of payments.

Unemployment

The forecasting of unemployment was very important, both because the amount of it was the most frequently used indicator of the amount of slack in the economy, or alternatively of strain on resources, present or prospective, and because of its often decisive political importance. But it was inherently very difficult; and in most NIF reports the forecasts of unemployment were put forward only with reserve. This was because experience showed that there was no constant relationship between changes in GDP and changes in the amount, or even in the direction, of unemployment. Even the last NIF report, of July 1964, said flatly

... the fact that we do not fully understand the relationship between changes in activity and changes in unemployment makes it hard to translate the forecast for the pressure of demand for goods and services into a forecast for the level of unemployment (though in fact their forecast that 'by mid-1965, unemployment, seasonally adjusted, may be barely 1.4 per cent' proved almost exactly right).

There were several reasons for this lack of constant relationship between the movements of GDP and those of unemployment. A change of demand and production has its direct impact on employment, not on unemployment. The numbers of employees in Great Britain, as measured by the mid-June counts of the Ministry of Labour, rose in every year from 1959 to 1964 by amounts ranging from 129,000 in 1963 to 383,000 in 1960; in 1958 there was a small fall. But the total workforce was growing all the time by natural increase, immigration, transfers from self-employment; and when demand was strong it was also swollen by an influx of part-timers and retired persons (of a total increase of 383,000 from June 1959 to June 1960 232,000 were women). Only a part, and a very variable part, of the increase in employment was met from a reduction of the numbers unemployed. In 1959/60, for instance, unemployment fell by only 108,000 against the increase of 383,000 in employment; and in 1961/62 a rise of 131,000 in those unemployed was accompanied by an almost equal *growth* in employment. Only in 1963/64 did the fall in unemployment slightly exceed the rise in the total number of employees.

Apart from this difficulty, there was not in fact a simple correlation between change in GDP and in *employment*. The former rose usually more than the latter, because of the growth of production per person employed, though there were exceptions: between the second quarters of 1961 and 1962 employment rose by *more* than GDP (1.4 per cent against 1.0 per cent), and in 1957/58 it seems to have fallen slightly *less* than GDP. And in the other years the relationship was erratic, with GDP increasing much faster than employment in the upswing of 1959/60 and again in 1962/63 and 1963/64, but by little more than employment in 1960/61. Over the whole period the growth in production per person employed was 19.3 per cent, giving an annual cumulative rate of 3 per cent a year. Therefore on *average* GDP must grow at least at that rate if unemployment were to be reduced, but the actual relationship from year to year was erratic.

The forecasters generally used a formula, mentioned already, which in effect allocated about 3.25 per cent of annual forecast growth of GDP to covering growth of the labour force and productivity, and any excess or deficiency on this to reduction or increase of unemployment. But they were conscious that there could be a large resultant error. They attributed this mainly to the apparent tendency of employers to hold on for some time to mere labour than they really needed when demand slackened unexpectedly (as in late 1960), and then to shake it out quickly when they lost confidence in the prospects of further growth for some time ahead (as in 1962). Thereafter, streamlining of methods and the maturing of labour-saving investment enabled them to meet the first impact of reviving demand, when it came, without immediate re-engagement of labour; this came at the second stage of expansion of demand. This explanation seems to fit the actual course of events during this period; but to apply it successfully to the forecast growth of GDP, even if this were correct, would have required a better diagnosis of starting levels and trends than the forecasters were able to make.

Forecasts of unemployment were thus doubly uncertain: the forecasts of GDP might be wrong and, whether they were or not, the movements of unemployment might not bear the expected relationship to them. But they had to be attempted. The forecasts of unemployment made are compared as far as possible with the eventual outcome in the table below.

Unemployment: forecast and actual

Date of report	Forecast	Actual (total registered in GB)
12.12.58	Rising early 1959, then level	1958 III/1959 I: rise of 73,000; 1959 I/1959 IV: fall of 161,000
28.5.59	1958 IV/1959IV: fall of 100,000	Fall of 86,000
10.12.59	1959 IV/1960 IV: fall of 50-60,000	Fall of 74,000
9.2.60	1959 IV/1960 IV: fall of 100,000	Fall of 74,000
9.6.60	1960 1st half/1961 first half: no change	Fall of 50,000
12.12.60	Autumn 1960/autumn 1961: rise of 80,000	Rise of 31,000 1960 IV/1961 IV
9.3.61	No substantial change over 1961	Rise of 24,000 Dec 60/Dec 61
14.6.61	Pressure increasing: fall to 1955 levels (c.1.3%) by first half	1961 1st half/62 1sthalf: rise of 154,000 (0.9%)
15.11.61	Rise of 90,000 1961 II/1962 I, thereafter no change, except seasonal fall to 350,000 mid-year. Average 1962 1.8%.	Rise of 180,000; 400,000 mid-1962; rise to 537,000 in Dec. Av. 1962 2.0%
20.2.62	1962 I/1963 II. Possible rise at first, but falling by 1963 I to perhaps 400,000	1962 I/II, seasonal fall of 32,000: then rapid rise to 798,000 1963 I.

6.7.62	1962 II/1963 II: some further rise to 475,000 in January/February 1963, falling to 400,000 by mid-year	Rise of 142,000 May/Dec and on to 843,000 total on Jan/Fen (hard winter); 490,000 in Jun/Jul 1963.
30.11.62	1962 III/1963 III. Probably little change, but uncertain how long labour shakeout will continue	Rise of 52,000
19.2.63	Year 1963: moderate further rise in 1st half, then at least no fall.	1963. Rise of 312,000 Dec/Feb (hard winter); then fall. Dec 62/Dec 63, fall of 100,000.
10.7.63	'Particularly uncertain'. ?1963 II/1964 II, fall of 100,000 to below 2% by mid-64	Fall of 178,000, 1.4% June/July 1964.
13.11.63	'The forecast change in capacity utilisation is worth a fall of 100,000' - to 1.7% by mid-Oct 64, but uncertain	Fall of 126,000, Oct 63/Oct 64, to 1.5%.
11.2.64	1963 III/1965 I: fall of 170,000, from 2.3% to 1.5% (seasonally adjusted)	Fall of 200,000 to 1.4%
1.7.64	'By mid-1965, unemployment, seasonally adjusted, may be barely 1.4%'	Jun/Jul 65 actual 1.2%, adjusted 1.3%.

It will be seen that the errors and successes in the forecasts of unemployment followed fairly closely those in the forecasts of GDP, despite the forecasters' own doubts about the finer points of the relationship between them. In the two periods of expansion, for the first years, 1959 and 1963, they rightly predicted a fall in unemployment, but greatly @BODY TEXT = underestimated its amount. For the second years, 1960 and 1964, they came close to the actual results, though only with some help from changes of Government policy after the forecasts were made. For 1961, and still more for 1962, they were badly at sea.

Comparison of the timing of actual movements of unemployment with those of GDP on the whole supports the forecasters' views about the relationship between them. GDP rose at more than 3 per cent a year from the fourth quarter of 1958 to the first quarter of 1960, possibly in the first quarter of 1961 and in the second quarter of 1962, and clearly from the second quarter of 1963 through 1964. It actually fell slightly for most of 1958, and from the third quarter of 1961 to the first quarter of 1962, and again in the fourth quarter and at the beginning of 1963. The curve of unemployment, seasonally adjusted, rose steadily from the autumn of 1957 to February 1959; but fell steadily to the spring of 1961. After hesitancy in the second quarter of that year, it rose continuously to March 1963, then fell rapidly to the end of 1964. Its downward turning points thus occurred two or three months after the beginning of substantial growth in GDP; but its upward turning point in 1961 lagged by about a year behind the flattening of the growth of GDP below 3 per cent in the summer of 1960. The beginning of the rise in unemployment may have been delayed by the resumed build-up of activity in the first half of 1961, but once started, its pace was not even checked by the temporary recovery of demand in the middle of 1962.

Wages

The NIF reports also contained forecasts of the rate of increase of wages, as represented by movements of either the hourly or the weekly wage index, and of the growth of total income from employment. This differed from the rate of increase of wages because it included some allowance for 'wage drift', changes in salaries, and – most important – the effect of expected changes in employment. The forecasts given in the November/December reports are compared with what is now believed to have been the actual outturn are compared in the table below. Comparisons based on the February and June reports do not give a significantly different picture, though that of June 1961, just before the 'wage pause', predicted a rise of 6.5 per cent to June 1962, against an outturn of only about 5.5 per cent

It will be seen that, except for 1959, the forecasts consistently understated the amounts of the increases in weekly or hourly wage rates, the differences being particularly serious for 1961 and 1962. The growth of income from employment was also generally, though less markedly, understated in the forecasts. The extreme case of understatement was, curiously enough, 1959, when the forecast rise of wage rates was much *greater* than the reality: in the event, 'wage drift' and the large but unforeseen rise in employment much more than offset the overestimate of the rise in rates. In 1962, the opposite happened: the rise in wage rates was under-forecast, but the failure of the economy to grow as much as was expected offset this, so that the forecast increase in total income from employment was not far wrong. The forecast for 1963, with a small understatement of the rise in wage rates and a rather larger understatement of the growth in total employment income, came nearest to the recorded facts.

Prices

The increases in wage rates and income from employment discussed above were, of course, in money terms. Before they could be incorporated in the forecasts of the growth of GDP in real terms (at 1954 or 1958 prices) they had to be deflated by an estimate of the price increases expected in the forecast period. This also figures in the reports in its own right. The forecasted and actual changes in the index of retail (and sometimes of consumer) prices are compared below. Since changes in indirect taxation had quick effects on the retail price index, the forecasts made in both the November/December and the post-budget reports are shown.

Retail or consumer price index: Forecast and actual (percentage increases)

Date of report	Period covered	Forecast	Actual
12.12.58	Change 1959 on 1958	2.0% (retail)	0.5% (retail)
28.5.59	1959 II/IV	No higher than a year earlier, because of tax cuts	0.3%
10.12.59	1960	1.5%	2.1%

9.6.60	1960 1st half/61 2nd half	2%	2.6%
12.12.60	1960 III/1961 IV	3%	5.2%
14.6.61	1961 1st half/ 1962 1st half	3%/3.5%	4.0%
15.11.61	1961 IV/1962 IV/1963 I	2.25%	Fall 0.5% Rise 0.7%
6.7.62	May 62/May 63	Fall May/Sep 62, 1.5% Rise Oct 62/May 63 to prev. level	1.4% (consumer)
30.11.62	1962 III/1963 III	1.5% (consumer)	2.7% (consumer)
10.7.63	1963 II/1964 II	2.0% (consumer)	4.1% (consumer)
13.11.63	1964	2.0% or less (consumer)	2.5% (64 II/65 I)
1.7.64	May 64/early 65	2.0% or more (consumer)	

The rise in retail or consumer prices, both forecast and actual, was continuous throughout the period, except for a short time in the summer of 1962; but the rate of increase varied considerably. Except in 1959 and in the winter and spring of 1962/63, the forecasters considerably underestimated it. This underestimation was particularly marked when the pressure on resources was high, as from the second half of 1960 to early 1962 and again in the summer and autumn of 1964. It has already been suggested that this was one of the reasons why consumer demand failed in these periods to grow as fast as was forecast. It also had, along with the general 'real terms' focus of the forecasts, an unfortunate effect in disguising from officials and Ministers the amount of monetary inflation which was actually going on.

Comment

Criticism of the Treasury forecasts with the help of hindsight is necessarily invidious. No detailed comparison has been made between them and other contemporary appraisals, such as those of the NIESR; but it does not appear that any of these were notably more successful. The methods of forecasting used by the Treasury were refined and developed during the period, and it is fair to note that the forecasts made from the end of 1962 onwards were rather more successful (after allowing for budgetary changes made after the forecasts themselves) than most of the earlier ones. Nevertheless, the forecasts were generally an inadequate, and sometimes a very misleading, guide for the policy of control of demand.

The main weaknesses which stand out may be summarised as follows:

1. Failure to make a correct appraisal of the current, or very recent, level and trend of activity. This was present throughout, though it was most marked in the early and middle years. It seems to have been mainly due to lack of up-to-date information, especially about industrial production and investment.

2. Inability to measure changes in 'business confidence' and expectations and to apply their effects to the forecasts. This seems to have been the main reason for the failure to

predict the very rapid pace of expansion in 1959 and in 1963 (though unexpectedly large exports played some part here).

3. Of changes in the amount of stocks and work in progress the forecasters always felt uncertain. The causes were complex; the amount of up-to-date information was very small; and even today the figures available for the years 1958 to 1964 probably have a large margin of error. But it is clear that the rise in imported stocks was the main cause of the failure of the import forecasts in 1960 and in 1964, and changes in home-produced stocks and work in progress were certainly wrongly forecast both then and in some other years. Since, very broadly, a 3 per cent change in this item could affect GDP by about 1 per cent, the effects of a bad forecast of it on the whole picture could be large.

4. Correct forecasting of exports is obviously very difficult because their amount depends on movements of world demand as well as on the ability of home production to meet them. Errors in the export forecasts were most important for 1959, the second half of 1962, and for 1963, both directly and because of their consequential effects. A rise in exports both increases incomes and therefore home demand and diminishes the supplies available to meet it, thereby stimulating a further rise in production; a fall in exports has the opposite effect.

5. Most of the forecasts understated the future rise of wages and prices. This probably caused them to overstate the rise of demand and GDP in real terms, as well as minimising the amount of monetary inflation.

6. The practice of summarising the forecasts mainly in terms of the movements of final expenditure and of GDP expressed in terms of constant and much out-of-date price-levels (1954 to mid-1962, 1958 thereafter), facilitated comparison of expected and past rates of growth. But it distracted attention from the monetary changes involved, which it was one of the Government's purposes to control. It sometimes led to simple misunderstandings: the minutes of the Budget Committee show several cases where forecast figures of consumers' expenditure in real terms were carried directly into discussions of the appropriate amount of budgetary changes, which were of course, expressed in current money terms. It is true that from the end of 1962 current price tables were prepared and were added to the usual forecast tables in terms of 1958 prices. But they were given a narrow separate circulation and were not referred to in the reports themselves.

Notes on the 'regulator'

As has already been recorded (pp. 22-25), the Finance Act 1961 gave to the Chancellor power to impose by Treasury Order a surcharge, not exceeding 4s a week, on the employers' contributions for National Insurance; and either a surcharge or a rebate, not exceeding 10 per cent, on all Customs and Excise duties. The first power met with much criticism in Parliament. It was never used, and the power to use it was dropped from the Finance Act 1962. The second was used to its full extent upwards as one of the measures of July 1961, and the power was retained, with some modifications, in successive Finance Acts. But it was not again applied, either upwards or downwards, in the period to October 1964. Since it was originally introduced as a primary instrument for controlling the economy, it is worth examining why it was not used more often, despite several apparently favourable opportunities.

The Customs and Excise surcharge was imposed, at the full 10 per cent, as a crisis measure in July 1961. It was expected to withdraw purchasing power at the rate of £210 million a year, beginning immediately. About £80 million of this would come from the duties on tobacco, £40 million each from those on alcohol and oil (including fuel oil largely used in industry), and £35 million from purchase tax on a wide range of goods taxed at rates varying from 50 to 5 per cent. For the first three categories, tax was already a large part of the final price to the consumer, so that a 10 per cent surcharge meant, when it was passed on, a substantial increase; for cheap goods subject to the lower rate of purchase tax, levied on the wholesale value, the effect of the surcharge on retail prices would be almost imperceptible. But, despite its uneven impact, it would take away, mainly from final consumers, a sum equal to over 1 per cent of their total current spending.

The crisis passed quickly. Sterling recovered, demand was checked, unemployment rose and unfilled vacancies fell. It was therefore widely expected that the surcharge would be removed, either at the end of the year or in the budget of 1962. There were two reasons why this did not happen. First, official Treasury advice, both before Christmas and before the budget, was that continued restraint of home demand was necessary in order to leave room for a big rise in exports. Second, the rise of public expenditure had not been checked effectively by the July measures, and an increase of permanent taxation was needed to cover it. In 1961/62 expenditure above and below the line had exceeded the budget estimates by £180 million, and the overall deficit had been £211 million instead of £69 million, even with the help of eight months receipts from the surcharge; and for 1962/63 expenditure, despite the Chancellor's undertaking of July, was expected to show a further increase of £250 million. It would, of course, have been possible to remove the surcharge and to replace the loss of revenue by an increase of direct taxation, but this would have conflicted with the Government's general fiscal objectives. Another possibility for the budget and the Finance Bill was to renew the existing powers and retain the surcharge – and the revenue from it – on a temporary basis. This would permit reductions of up to 20 per cent (removal of surcharge, and rebate) if reflation became necessary, but no further increase in 1962 if yet more restraint of demand were needed. It would also fail to cover the increase of public expenditure on a 'permanent' basis. Probably for the two last reasons, it does not seem to have been canvassed within the Treasury. It was therefore accepted from an early stage[1] in the preparations for the budget of 1962 that the 'crisis' surcharge should be embodied in permanent increases in broadly the same duties, and that the power to use the regulator, up or down, should be renewed so as to apply to these higher rates. The Chancellor took credit in his budget speech for the fact he would thus retain the power to reduce them – to about the pre-crisis rates but not lower – if need should arise. But when, on 23 June 1962, he came under pressure from his colleagues to reflate the economy, he told Sir Frank Lee[2] that if this had to be done he would not wish to use the regulator downwards, or to increase public expenditure, because either course would raise the overall budget deficit. The course of consolidation adopted in the budget of 1961 brought out sharply the fundamental difficulty of keeping the regulator as a cyclical instrument isolated from other budgetary considerations. It was probably the best in the circumstances, but it did not inspire much public confidence in the regulator as a beneficient instrument of control.

Use of the regulator in reverse, by rebate, was in the list of possible reflationary measures presented to the new Chancellor, Mr Maudling, on 17 July 1962. But it was accompanied by advice, which he accepted, to take no immediate action. A fortnight later, when opinion in the Treasury had shifted, immediate use of the regulator was discussed by officials. But there was by then no time left in which to get the necessary decisions and to lay a Treasury Order for the rebate before the House rose for the recess: and after that, the requirement that the Order must be confirmed within 21 calendar days ruled out the use of the regulator until early October, unless the House were to be specially recalled.

There were in any case other objections. In a discussion with Mr Cairncross the Chancellor said that early use of the regulator would make the framing of the 1963 budget much more difficult. He would prefer to do something to reduce industrial costs or to encourage investment. When this was reported to the Budget Committee on 2 August, opinions were divided.[3] Mr Cairncross championed the use of the regulator as the primary instrument as soon as the need for reflation was clear, arguing that a stimulus to consumption would be the best way of encouraging investment. Sir Richard Powell and, on the whole, Sir Frank Lee, disliked the idea of starting a consumption boom, because of possibly adverse effects on exports; they sympathised with the Chancellor's desire to reduce costs and stimulate investment directly, though they had no great faith in changing depreciation allowances or removing the duty on fuel oil, which were the means he had indicated for doing this. Other members favoured a regulator rebate on the grounds that it would help wages policy by reducing consumer prices and offsetting some of the recent increases which were resulting from the Government's stiffer pricing policy for nationalised industries. But Sir James Crombie, for Customs and Excise, thought that few prices would be reduced, at least in the short run. The effects of a rebate would not be simply the opposite of a surcharge. It was easy to pass on a surcharge imposed at a time of strong demand. But, with a rebate, most manufacturers would wait for it to be overtaken by cost increases instead of reducing their prices; and for retailers there was always the problem of tax-paid stocks, which they would in any case try to work off before reducing prices. This was particularly likely to happen where a 10 per cent rebate of tax could only be a very small proportion of the final price, as for articles subject only to the lower rates of purchase tax. A rebate might help profits, but would not, directly, much affect final demand. The majority of the Budget Committee were against using the regulator in reverse at that time.

This majority view was reported to the Chancellor[4] during meetings on 10 and 12 September, when the 'October measures' were taking shape. Sir Frank Lee nonetheless suggested that preparations might be made for a 5 per cent rebate, to show the Government's willingness to make some contribution to keeping prices down. The Chancellor replied that, if he used the regulator at all, it would be at 10 per cent; but, after reserving his decision for a few days, he decided against its inclusion in the measures which were announced on 2 October. When the unemployment figures worsened later in the month, Mr Cairncross again pressed for the use of the regulator to its fullest extent, but he received little support. Instead, the Budget Committee recommended[5] for announcement on 5 November the immediate reduction by Treasury Order of the purchase tax on cars from 45 to 25 per cent: this would have a noticeable, if concentrated, effect on prices and demand. Similar treatment was given to the other higher rates of purchase tax at the end of the year. The Chancellor himself, against advice, promised immediate increases in investment allowances, which would be ratified in due course in the Finance Act 1963.

The 'sweet simplicity' of the regulator as a reflationary weapon was thus deliberately discarded in favour of more selective stimuli. In the light of these experiences the future of the regulator was reviewed by a Working Group under the chairmanship of Mr Cairncross, and its report[6] was considered by the Budget Committee and the Chancellor in January 1963. The Group concluded that the arguments against using the regulator downward at that time were not reasons for abandoning the power to use it in future. It recommended that the powers should be renewed by the Finance Act so as to permit both upward and downward use; and that, if possible, the 'calendar days' requirement for the confirmation Treasury Orders under them should be converted to the more usual 'sitting days', so as to make it possible to use the powers at any time during a Parliamentary recess. It might help to get agreement to this change if the procedure for making Treasury Orders on purchase tax were assimilated to that for the regulator. In the last resort, the change to 'sitting days' might be applied only to downward movements, since there was less constitutional objection to remission of taxation by Order than to making additions to it. The Group also recommended that the scope of the regulator should remain unchanged and that its unity should be preserved, despite suggestions from the previous Chancellor that its use might be easier if surcharges or rebates could be applied selectively and at differential rates to the various duties, so as to meet political criticism of, for example, a reduction of surcharge on tobacco just after a strong Committee had reported on the dangers of smoking. The Chancellor accepted all the recommendations at the time. But in the Finance Bill 1963 the change to 'sitting days' was in fact restricted to downward movements; and in the following year, in order to make more acceptable an increase in the permanent duties on drink and tobacco, he took power to exclude from a surcharge or rebate one or more of the four major blocks of duties – on tobacco, oil, alcohol, purchase tax – though the rates of surcharge or rebate for those groups which were taxed must remain uniform.

In the New Year 1963 more reflation was still felt to be needed, and the opportunity to use the regulator downwards still existed. At a meeting of the Budget Committee on 7 January[7] Mr Cairncross again advocated this, preferably before the budget. But it was known that the Chancellor intended to concentrate any further concessions mainly on direct taxation, and no one disputed Sir William Armstrong's comment that, at least in a budget, income tax could be a good regulator. No one at that time foresaw the early need, which became apparent before the end of the year, once again to *check* the growth of demand. This might have been done sooner and more easily if some of the budget concessions had been made on an avowedly temporary basis by means of the regulator. Presentationally, there was some difference between removing a rebate and imposing either surcharge or more permanent taxation, as was in fact done in the 1964 budget.

Another use of the regulator upwards did indeed come to the fore as one of the possibilities for the budget of 1964 and after it. By February, none doubted that demand must be checked, and the Chancellor felt none of the inhibitions about using it upwards which had prevented him from using it downwards.[8] But, as in 1962, the rapid growth of public expenditure made an increase of ordinary taxation preferable, if politically possible; and in any case the regulator might be needed as well, later in the year. Therefore a regulator surcharge was suggested as part of the budget only if the prospect of a spring election made it necessary to keep the Finance Bill short and uncontroversial.[9] When this prospect was removed, it suited the Government's general policy both to steady demand and to cover expenditure by raising an extra £100 million by higher ordinary taxation of drink and tobacco, while renewing the regulator powers in more flexible form ready for another dose later if required.

In July, when the Budget Committee considered that some further restraint of demand was needed, they discussed the use of these powers to impose, before the summer recess, a surcharge on the oil duties and on purchase tax. But they did not recommend it,[10] judging that, though it would impose a significant restraint on the growth of demand, it would be a shock to opinion which might deter investment decisions important for the future growth of the economy. Moreover, they thought that demand for consumer durables subject to purchase tax was not growing excessively at that time, while a surcharge on oil would be attacked as raising costs. Their preferred alternative, a call for special deposits from the banks, was, however, not accepted by the Chancellor, and no action at all was taken. The regulator was of course again used by the next Government in 1966 and 1968.

The history of the regulators from their inception in 1961 down to October 1964 thus provides more evidence about the difficulties of using them at all than about their efficacy, if used, for controlling demand. Political criticism slew the Insurance surcharge regulator at birth; and the Government's general desire to shift the balance towards indirect taxation underlay the unwillingness of the Chancellors to remove the first Customs and Excise surcharge in 1961 or to use the power to rebate later. In addition, although the magnitudes involved were not clearly worked out until about 1963, the upward trend of public expenditure had become steeper than that of the yield of taxation at unchanged rates. This created pressures, felt in 1962 and 1964, to make increases of taxation in permanent rather than temporary form. The logical counterpart, however, that when reductions were made for stimulatory reasons. they had better be temporary rather than permanent (and should not mortgage the distant future as investment allowances did) was not attended to. In general, the idea that an economic fiscal regulator could be operated not merely outside the budget but largely independently of ordinary budgetary considerations was proved to be impracticable.

The application of the Customs and Excise surcharge in July 1961 was only one part of a considerable package. It is therefore not easy to isolate its actual effects on demand in order to see whether they came up to expectations. The 10 per cent surcharge was expected to yield revenue at the rate of £200–210 million a year, the bulk of which would come from alcohol, tobacco and oil. It was assumed that it would be passed on very quickly in increased prices to consumers. Since the price elasticity of demand for these things was certainly low, general consumer demand would be reduced mainly because the buyers of them would have less to spend on other things. The Economic Section assessed the net effect on final demand at £140 million (including perhaps £30 million of imports), the difference of £60 million representing a maintenance of demand from a reduction of savings. The July measures as a whole checked the growth of total demand and production more in the short term than had been expected and it is not possible to be sure from the out-turn figures now available (which may themselves have a margin of error) how much the regulator surcharge alone contributed to this. Consumer demand itself does not seem to have been rising very fast before the July measures – only about £100 million in money terms and much less at constant prices in the first half of 1961. In the second half of the year its growth in money terms continued at the same rate, while in real terms it became practically stationary; in both, however, there was a big spurt in the first half of 1962. It seems that consumers took a very large part of the shock of price increases, both those induced by the surcharge and others, by reducing their savings rather than their expenditure; personal savings, after rising by £100 million in the first half of 1961, fell by £30 million in the second half and by a further £100 million in the first half of 1962. It looks as if the regulator itself may have played a smaller part in steadying the economy in 1961 than was thought at the time. It was also an inherent weakness in the surcharge that it operated by raising prices rather than by reducing disposable incomes. At a time when a major Government objective was to reduce the pressure for wage increases, this was an aspect which deserved more attention than it received within the Treasury.

Since the regulator was not used in reverse during this period, there is no evidence about its efficiency as an economic stimulator. Discussion of its possible use in the autumn of 1962 did, however, bring out some important points. The belief of Customs and Excise that a rebate would be passed on in the prices of the taxed goods less and more slowly than a surcharge may well have been correct; and the resultant improvement in the profits of manufacturers and distributors of goods, demand for which was mostly inelastic, would not be a very quick stimulator of production. It is also possible that, if price reductions in these goods did take place, they would in the short run raise the rate of consumer's savings more than their expenditure on other goods. It may well be that really sizeable reductions in purchase tax, concentrated on goods of elastic demand, which was the device finally adopted in the autumn of 1962, was a more effective stimulant than a regulator rebate would have been, even though the total amount of revenue foregone thereby was much smaller. These reductions had an immediate impact on both consumers and producers. It is, however, obviously easier politically to make large selective changes of this kind downwards than upwards.

It was remarked several times that changes in the rate of income tax, bearing directly on disposable incomes of all kinds, might well be the most efficient regulator, if means could be found of applying them quickly inside the financial year. The idea was briefly examined during the original search for suitable regulators in 1960, and more work was done on it in 1961, without positive result.[11] The PAYE machinery seemed at first sight to give an easy entry. But the idea met with implacable resistance from the Inland Revenue, who felt that their task of assessing and collecting income tax and surtax was heavy enough without added complications; and no one was able to shake their arguments that these would be very great. The central difficulty was that individual codings for PAYE were adapted to the personal circumstances of each taxpayer (allowances for wife and children, for past over-or-under payments, etc. as well as to earnings.) These could be, and many were, altered during the financial year. But to alter them all at once was an enormous task. It took the Inland Revenue about three months to make even budget changes operative for PAYE, so that a 'regulator' change of rates could not be made to bite quickly and would require additional staff. If an attempt were made to simplify it by applying a flat percentage addition or deduction to all codings, with final settlement at the end of the year, all sorts of hardships and further complications would arise. There were also difficulties about classes of income which were not subject to PAYE. Dividend payments, for which tax was deducted at source, were related to company profits in years which ended at different dates; fair decisions about what should be subject to surcharge and what not would be difficult. Parallel difficulties would arise about income from self-employment. Finally, most surtax was payable in a single lump on 1 January on the income accruing in the *previous* financial year, and surcharge or rebate could probably only apply in arrears. These objections seemed at the time to be insuperable. An ingenious plan was presented by Professor Phelps Brown to Sir Frank Lee which apparently aimed at advancing or retarding the dates of deduction or payment of tax ran into rather similar troubles.[12] Some of the difficulties of devising a means of making quick changes arose from the great complexity of the income tax allowance, differences of treatment between classes of income, and the division between income tax and surtax; with a simpler system, something both equitable and administratively practicable could probably be devised. But it is in any case probable that, during this period, the Government would not have been prepared to legislate for a form of regulator which provided for even temporary increases in direct personal taxation.

Notes

1   BC minutes, 2.11.61; BC (M) (62) 8, 23.2.62.
2   2 EAS/1/04. Hubback to Lee, 26.6.62.
3   BC minutes, 2.8.62.
4   BC (63) 04. Notes on meetings with Chancellor, 10 and 12.9.62.
5   BC (63) 03. Armstrong to Chancellor, 15 and 24.10.62.
6   BC (M) (63) 4, covering BC (62) 39 and BC (63) 2.
7   BC minutes, 7.1.63.
8   BC (64) 04. Note of discussion with the Chancellor, 19.2.64.
9   BC (M) (64) 3, 20.2.64.
10 BC (M) (64) 4.
11 BC minutes, 15.6.60; BC (61) 33, November 61.
12 BC (62) 03A, October 61.

Summary and conclusions

From 1958 to 1964 the policy of control of demand was moderately successful. It kept the fluctuations of the economy within narrow limits. It did this with an average rate of growth which, though disappointing by contrast with that of other developed countries, was at least higher than that which went before and after. An average rate of registered unemployment of 1.9 per cent, though higher than in previous post-war years, did not indicate an intolerable under-use of resources. Crises for sterling, though not avoided, were fairly easily remedied in the short term. The policy failed to stop the inflation of wage costs and prices and at times probably aggravated it; but it now seems clear that control of demand alone could not have provided the remedy.

Nevertheless, even for its primary object of keeping the growth of the economy steady, the policy could clearly have been better executed. Restraints on demand were kept on too long in 1958 and 1962. Demand was allowed, indeed, was encouraged, to expand too fast and too far in 1959 and 1963. The problem of transition from too rapid expansion to steady growth was not solved, either in 1960 and 1961 or in 1964. The reasons for over-stimulation of the economy were largely political. The electoral cycle played a decisive part in 1959 and 1964; departmental pressures to increase public expenditure, which were a built-in expansionary force at all times, produced excessive results whenever the brakes were relaxed; the nervousness of ministers about winter and regional unemployment encouraged the desire to run the whole economy at too high a level. But official Treasury advice was also at fault. The forecasters failed to foresee the changes to rapid expansion in 1959 and 1963, and then never fully recognised their force and cumulative momentum. For the critical budgets of 1959 and 1963 the advice of most officials was not for less than the Chancellors performed, and some officials suggested more. This was not true, however, when the brakes had to be put on again. In 1960, and still more in 1961, and again in 1964, officials would have liked sterner measures of restraint than those which were applied. The delay in beginning reflation in 1958 also owed something to political considerations; it was difficult, after Mr Thorneycroft's resignation as Chancellor in January, at once to seem to throw all his doctrines of restraint to the winds. But most Treasury advice, with an eye on the balance of payments, also moved very cautiously. In 1962 there was a bad failure of diagnosis and forecasting, complicated when this began to be realised by a change of Chancellors and by the onset of the summer Parliamentary recess. For the period as a whole the verdict seems to be: for reflation, too late, too much, continued too long; for restraint, not enough at first, and therefore drawn out and also continued too long.

Some of the hesitations, and also some of the excesses, both in reflation and in restraint, were also due to shifts of emphasis in the Government's avowed objectives for economic policy. Early in the period the public focus was still heavily on maintaining the internal and external value of the pound. As has been said, this delayed reflation in 1958 and gave the decisive impulse for the deflationary 'package' of July 1961, which was very considerable if not as large as officials pressed for. Later 'growth' and 'modernisation of Britain' were the watch-words, and, after the establishment of the NEDC the Government committed itself against almost all official advice to a growth of 4 per cent as the annual norm. The trouble about this was that it could be sustained only, if at all, with the help of big changes in the efficiency of management and the attitude of labour, which at best would take some years to achieve; yet in the meantime the Government was deterred in 1964 (and its successor later) from taking measures to limit the growth of demand to a lower rate appropriate to the actual condition of the economy. Finally, there was the old commitment, and the continuous pressure, for 'full employment'. But how full was 'full'? The Treasury forecasters and economists thought that a national (seasonally adjusted) average of 1.7 per cent (rather lower early in the period) of unemployment was the minimum, below which the economy became overheated. But this average covered much higher figures in depressed areas, in declining occupations, and during winter; so the uninformed public thought it too high. On the other hand, it also covered lower figures of unemployment, especially of skilled workers, in many industries and services and in many places, especially, but not only, in the south east and the Midlands. The economy had always too much slack in the skirt, but was frequently too tight in the waist. In retrospect, its behaviour in 1960 and 1961, and again in 1964 and later, strongly suggests that the Treasury danger points of 1.5–1.7 per cent unemployment were in fact set too low, given the uneven distribution of labour and plant capacity in relation to the calls on it when pressure of demand rose fast and high.

Successful control of demand requires correct appraisal of the level and trend of demand and activity at the time of the forecast, ability to spot and assess the forces making for changes of trend or pace in the period of the forecast, and a proper evaluation of the effects on the whole economy of Government measures of reflation or deflation: and all this, be it emphasised, within limits of accuracy which are very narrow in relation to demand and national output as a whole. It cannot be surprising that the forecasts were often wrong – occasionally, as in 1962, in direction, usually more or less in degree. Weakness in current appraisal was mainly due to inadequacy, lateness, and unreliability of the information available. The quantity of information was much increased during the period, and many more indicators came into use; but, as appeared in the summer of 1964, the problem of combining promptitude with reliability was not solved and probably too much attention was paid to month-by-month assessments based on information which had later to be revised. For forecasting itself, forward information about investment intentions, the state of order books, building starts, was improved, and more elaborate methods were used to take account of cumulative and multiplier effects. The forecasting of stock changes remained, however, very speculative; and even in the last report of the period the forecasters admitted that they did not fully understand the relation between changes in GDP and in the amount of unemployment. The forecasts made in the last twelve months were in fact more successful than any of those earlier in the period, but they were still an imperfect and uncertain guide for policy. Assessment of the probable quantitative effects of proposed measures of control was rudimentary early in the period, and not elaborate even at the end: not until early 1964 were systematic attempts made to estimate the effects of possible budgetary changes over periods of time, and no one even tried to guess at the quantitative effects of particular monetary measures on consumers' demand or on investment. Throughout, the fact that the appraisals and forecasts were expressed in terms of constant prices diverted attention from the monetary inflation which was taking place and sometimes caused confusion about the money value of the budgetary and other measures which were needed.

Several new instruments for controlling demand were introduced during the period. Repayment of post-war credits was used as a reflationary measure in the budget of 1959 and again in November 1962. This did not come up to expectations. The repayments claimed were much less than was expected, and it is likely that much of them was invested and not added quickly to current demand. In April 1960 the Bank of England made a call for 'special deposits' from the joint-stock banks as a means of checking the growth of bank lending. This device had been negotiated in 1958 as the price for the removal of the previous ceilings imposed on bank advances. It was used again in June 1960 and in July 1961, and proposed, but not used, in July 1964; and it certainly proved a useful check. But it had to be supplemented in July 1961 by the reintroduction of directives to the joint-stock banks setting priority categories for their lending and, after 1964, by the reintroduction of the ceilings themselves. All these were essentially means of restricting credit without raising interest rates (or raising them less), thus protecting the price of Government securities and, it was hoped, the level of industrial investment. The releases of 'special deposits', which were made in May, September and November 1962, were probably necessary conditions for reflation rather than stimuli in themselves. The next innovation in the fiscal field, the 'regulator' for which powers were taken in the Finance Act of 1961, was intended to give the Government a more flexible control over demand than could be provided by changes in taxation made only in annual, or emergency second, budgets. One part of it, the surcharge on employers' national insurance contributions, provoked so much hostility that it was never used, and the power to use it was dropped next year. The other part, the power to make a surcharge or rebate on all Customs and Excise duties, was in this period used only once upward, in July 1961, and never downward. As part of the reflationary measures of November 1962 another innovation, the use of Treasury powers to make by Order big selective reductions in purchase tax, was used instead, with the intention of giving a more concentrated stimulus to consumer spending and to particular forms of industrial production. Finally, the budget of 1963 gave for the first time the right of 'free depreciation' – freedom for firms to charge against taxable profits in any year the whole amount of the allowances for depreciation on new plant and machinery. This privilege was, however, restricted to investment within the Development Districts, and it was thus not so much a stimulus to investment in general (though it probably had some additive effect) as an attempt to influence its location by increasing the inducements already provided for investment there by the outright grants given by the Board of Trade.

Much attention was given in the period to the use of fiscal devices in the control of private investment, though this was one-sided because of the widely held view that most forms of industrial investment deserved special encouragement quite apart from cyclical considerations. But the instruments actually used – the grant of initial allowances for plant, machinery and buildings in 1958, with increases in the rates of allowance in November 1962, and of investment allowances in 1959 – had been used before. Inland Revenue opinion, and most Treasury opinion except that of some of the economists, was sceptical of their efficiency as a stimulus to investment unless market prospects were believed to justify this in any case, and it was dangerously slow-acting. As things turned out, the timing chosen was, with the possible exception of the reintroduction of initial allowances in 1958, wholly wrong; any stimulus actually given by the measures of 1959 and November 1962 can have materialised in actual expenditure on investment only in 1960/61 and 1964, when there was already too much without it.

Cyclical variation of public expenditure, and especially of investment, by the Government, local authorities, and the public corporations, was regarded by most public opinion and by some ministers as a natural instrument of control. Few officials agreed with this; several reports during the period concluded that both cuts in authorised programmes and emergency additions to them must be too slow to affect actual expenditure, besides usually involving disruption of the flow of orders and increased costs. But the pressure for public investment to rise was so strong that the Treasury welcomed opportunities to reduce it at any time. During crises of restraint, as in September 1957, early 1960, and July 1961, they managed to cut the programmes; when reflation was the policy they could not prevent large additional authorisations, though they warned against them. Public investment was not, at least in the short term, a good weapon for dealing with even local unemployment, because with modern methods of construction so much of the money was spent outside the affected areas and inflated demand mainly in the rest of the economy. The tighter five-year programming machinery developed by the Treasury from 1962 onwards for public expenditure as a whole was intended to bring better order into this field; but it in fact coincided with the most rapid and ill-timed growth of public expenditure on investment during the period. For most of it the oscillations of policy achieved results which were the opposite of correct cyclical timing. Expenditure on investment in the public sector fell for most of 1958 and was stationary or falling in the summer and autumn of 1962; its large increase added to the too-rapid growth in 1959 and 1963; and it was still rising fast at the times of pressure in 1961 and 1964. Only in the first half of 1960 did it move downwards when restraint was needed. Except at that time its course coincided closely with that of investment expenditure in the private sector, and its variations were not much less violent. Reduction of public investment programmes may be a suitable remedy for prolonged overstrain of the economy, or their expansion for a prolonged deficiency of demand; but variations in them were not appropriate instruments to deal with the relatively short booms and recessions of the period.

The use of taxation as a whole as a means of controlling demand was affected by the rapid growth of public expenditure and by the attitude of the Government to the incidence of taxes. Public expenditure 'above the line' rose, on an outturn basis, by 47 per cent from 1958 to 1964. This was 3 per cent faster than the growth of GNP in money terms, and in the long run it clearly limited the remission of taxation. The tax system was, however, well geared for inflation because of its heavy reliance on progressive income tax and surtax, and over the period as a whole the remissions of taxation exceeded the increases – about £900 million against £600 million, without counting the effects of the concessions on investment allowances and 'free depreciation' which were made in 1963 but which affected the revenue mainly in 1965/66 onwards. Fears of 'budgeting for a deficit' did not in fact inhibit the amount of tax remissions when expansion was required in 1959 and 1963, though the budgetary need to match rising expenditure gave force to the economic arguments for restraint in 1962 and 1964. The Government was, however, committed to a policy of shifting the incidence from direct to indirect taxation, and this certainly had a large influence on the form taken by the remissions and increases. Over the whole period direct taxation was *reduced* by about £550 million (apart from the investment allowances and 'free depreciation'), and indirect taxation was *increased* by about £250 million. This shift had the unfortunate effect of generally raising prices; indeed, the usual indifference both of Treasury officials and of ministers to the choice between taking money out of the economy by raising prices or by reducing spendable incomes is one of the curious features of the story. But it was probably true that changes in indirect taxation had a more immediate effect on total demand, whether up or down.

Especially early in the period, ministers tried to shift the emphasis of control from fiscal to monetary measures, assisted by the new device of the call for 'special deposits' from the joint-stock banks, as well as by a more active use of changes in bank rate. But fear of discouraging long-term investment, as well as of making Government borrowing more expensive, limited the use of monetary measures when restraint was required; and as stimuli to expansion they were admittedly slow to act. Directives to the banks to discriminate in their lending against personal loans and in favour of exports were in force from July 1961 to November 1962. Hire purchase controls were used both for expansion and for restraint with considerable effect until June 1962, but they played no part later, though they were retained in existence at low rates. At the end of the period, as at the beginning, the budget remained the Government's chief and most effective instrument for the control of demand.